FORD
ESCORT RS

Twin-Cam; RS1600, 1800, 2000; Mexico

Osprey AutoHistory

FORD ESCORT RS

Twin-Cam; RS1600, 1800, 2000; Mexico

GRAHAM ROBSON

Published in 1981 by Osprey Publishing Limited,
12–14 Long Acre, London WC2E 9LP
Member company of the George Philip Group
First reprint winter 1982
Second reprint summer 1984
Third reprint spring 1985

United States distribution by

Osceola, Wisconsin 54020, USA

British Library Cataloguing in Publication Data

Robson, Graham
    Ford Escort RS.—(AutoHistory)
    1. Ford Escort automobile—History
    I. Title
    629.2′222   TL215.F7

ISBN 0-85045-401-8

Editor Tim Parker
Associate Michael Sedgwick
Photography Mirco Decet
Design Fred Price

Filmset and printed in England by
BAS Printers Limited, Over Wallop, Hampshire

Contents

Introduction

It would be too easy to suggest that the Ford RS Escorts need no introduction, for the individual cars themselves are well known. In some cases, however, their links with each other and with less specialised Ford models, are not. In this book my aim is to tell the integrated story of a very successful 12-year period in Ford's history, when a mass-production car maker was allowed the indulgence of building specialised models, in limited numbers.

Almost all the cars covered were sold in quantity: my only regret is that I am not able to quote accurate production figures. In the case of the Twin-Cam, for instance, the record of that period of manufacture at Halewood has never been made available and that of the AVO plant at South Ockendon has disappeared since the Rallye Sport division was closed down. Production of RS Escorts in Germany has not been released to me by Ford, not because they are ashamed of the numbers built (on the contrary, they are extremely proud of the success of the Mark II models) but because it is not their policy to encourage comparison between the productivity of British and German plants in the same group.

Throughout the book, therefore, some figures appear on the 'best guess' principle: other inferences can be drawn from the time it took for sporting homologation to be achieved for certain models and the Group into which the cars were listed.

Graham Robson

Chapter 1
Inventing a world-beater-the Boreham connection

Even in large, well-managed concerns, some success stories are unexpected. In the motor industry, it is possible to spend millions on a project, only to find that car buyers are not impressed. On the other hand—and it is so much more satisfying when it happens—a cheap and cheerful idea can sometimes result in a runaway winner.

If anyone at Ford ever tries to tell you that the Twin-Cam was a carefully planned product, don't believe them. Like so many other products which developed almost by chance, the Twin-Cam was one man's brainwave, a rush job, which eventually did more than was ever expected of it. The man was Henry Taylor, Ford's competitions manager in 1967, and the brainwave followed a sneak preview he had of company prototypes long after the product line-up had been decided.

The story really starts in 1961–62, when *Autocar*'s technical editor Harry Mundy, (a renowned ex-Coventry Climax engine designer), was commissioned by Colin Chapman to develop a twin-overhead-camshaft conversion for the Ford 'Kent' engine. This engine was specified for the Lotus Elan, announced in 1962 and for the Lotus-

Henry Taylor, Ford's Competitions Manager in 1967, who was the true 'father' of the Escort Twin-Cam, the first of the very successful Escort RS models

7

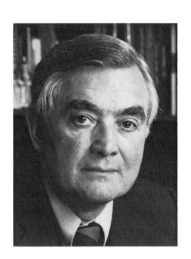

Left *Harry Mundy, who designed the original twin-cam engine conversion,* Centre *Colin Chapman, who first used it for the Elan and Lotus-Cortina models,* Right *Walter Hayes, Ford's public relations chief, who did so much to ensure that the Twin-Cam went into production*

Cortina, announced in 1963. Although the original Lotus-Cortinas were fragile and unreliable, much development by Lotus *and* Ford eventually turned them into exhilarating sports saloons. Not only was the engine refined into a deep-chested and very tuneable 1558 cc unit, but it was matched by well-developed gearbox and axle installations, and by suspension and braking systems to suit. Lotus assembled all the original-shape Lotus-Cortinas built between 1963 and 1966, but it was planned that the Mark II Lotus-Cortina—to be announced in March 1967—would be assembled at Dagenham.

In the meantime, Ford's world-wide policy had turned to a more aggressive involvement in motor sport. In Britain, the Ford competitions department directed by Walter Hayes, the company's public relations chief, had re-established itself in a new building at Boreham airfield in Essex: it was on the edge of the company's proving ground, where all the new and secret prototype models were tested, and had gone from strength to strength. First with Allan Platt as competition manager and then, (from 1965) under Henry Taylor, the department evolved from building class winners to constructing cars which could win outright, on tarmac, snow or in the loose, with or without practice.

Two factors then conspired to bring about the birth of an idea—the existing Lotus-Cortina went out of production in the autumn of 1966 and opposition from BMC, Alpine-Renault, Lancia and Porsche suddenly became more intense. There would be a long gap before the Mark II Lotus-Cortina could be homologated, and used by Henry Taylor's contracted drivers. As company policy decreed that obsolete models should not normally be raced or rallied, Taylor—and Boreham—were in for a quiet period in the winter of 1966–67.

It seems that, towards the end of 1966, Taylor and his chief mechanic Bill Meade, found time and interest to take a look at the activities of the Boreham test track, where the first, hand-built Ford Escorts were under development. It was probably Bill Meade who made the historic comment, 'Blimey, one of those things would go like hell with a Twin-Cam engine in it!' and his boss was quick to agree. But could it be done? And if it could, would anyone agree to build them in quantity? Taylor, who was not involved in the Monte Carlo Rally of January 1967, decided to find out. The new Escort was due to take over from the long-running Anglia in January 1968: with a year to go, could a truly fast derivative be developed and put on sale?

In big-company terms, what happened next was quite ludicrous for it ignored every known Ford procedure. Normally, to get approval for a new model at Ford, detailed engineering, production and finance plans have to be discussed, all manner of compromises have to be agreed, and the board of directors have to 'sign off' the project before a blow can be struck. But Henry Taylor

Bill Meade, Henry Taylor's chief mechanic at Boreham, Twin-Cam project linchpin in making it into a practical possibility

Bob Howe, a Ford product planner, who gave up his spare time to help turn Henry Taylor's bright idea into a feasible project

had no time for this—he thought he knew what sort of car he wanted and he thought he knew how it could be done. The formalities—the boring bits—could follow on at a later date!

Taylor, in effect, needed a new competition car—one which would be lighter and faster than the Lotus-Cortina, one that would still basically be a Ford and one that could be sold in sufficient quantities to ensure 'homologation' with the FIA for sporting use. It was the last requirement which was problematical. As far as a saloon car was concerned, Ford needed to make and sell at least 1000 examples in 12 consecutive months to compete in what was known as 'Group 2' against cars like the Mini-Cooper S, the Lancia Fulvia coupé, the Renault R8 Gordini and the Porsche 911. Lotus had already discovered how difficult it was to find that number of customers in a year for their Lotus-Cortinas; could Ford, with a smaller car, do at least as well?

Henry Taylor thought they could. After contacting Bob Howe of the Ford product planning division (who had been much involved with the concept of the 'ordinary' Escort), the two arranged a meeting at Henry Taylor's house in Wickham Bishops—not at his office at Boreham—one Sunday morning in January 1967. Henry and Bob produced the ideas, Peggy Taylor produced the coffee, and in a matter of hours the project had taken shape. The big problem then, was to sell it to management.

At this point, Henry Taylor knew only that he wanted to squeeze most of the Lotus-Cortina's mechanical components into the bodyshell and structure of the new Escort. He had no idea how this was to be done in reasonable quantities; he did not even know if it was physically possible, nor how much it would cost, and he had not really thought where and how such cars could be made.

All he could do was to ring up his boss, Walter Hayes, pour out his heart about the new scheme, and plead for his support.

Walter Hayes, in fact, was the right man, at the right time. It was he who had persuaded Ford's directors to put up £100,000 to back Keith Duckworth in the design of a four-cylinder Formula 2 engine (based on the Ford 'Kent' cylinder block) and of an entirely special 3-litre V8 Formula 1 engine. It was Hayes also, who had introduced Colin Chapman, and Lotus, to Ford in

The 'Mark I' Lotus-Cortina of 1963–66 used the Mundy-designed Twin-Cam engine, and was developed into a race and a rally winner. This was Allan Allard's privately owned example in the 1965 RAC Rally

the first place and the benefits were already beginning to work through. Hayes, of all people, could be relied upon to see the far-reaching implications of Henry Taylor's brainwave, and took to it immediately. The proposal between Taylor and Hayes was sewn up on 25 January 1967, from which the car's code name—J25—was derived.

Apart from the obvious problems—would the Lotus-Ford twin-cam engine, its gearbox and the back axle fit into the Escort's shell, and would the car be manageable?—there was the severely practical one regarding the Escort project itself. By the beginning of 1967 the design had been finalised, and huge amounts of money had been

The 'Mark II' Lotus-Cortina, built at Dagenham rather than by Lotus, was introduced in 1967, a year before the Escort Twin-Cam became available. The Twin-Cam used many Lotus-Cortina components

TERRY COLLINS

The original pushrod-engined Escort of 1968 was a simple little machine. The 1968-only reaction-strut front suspension can just be seen in this drawing

committed to the manufacture of tools to press the bodyshell panels, weld it all together, machine the new transmission parts, and for the re-equipment of the Halewood (Liverpool) production lines. It was at Halewood that the Escorts—saloons, vans and estate cars—were due to take the place of the Anglias towards the end of 1967.

There would be a wide range of different Escorts, but they would all have conventional Ford 'Kent' pushrod engines, the new small gearbox and 12-in road wheels. It seems incredible now, but there were no plans to make any Escort with an engine larger than 1297 cc, or with more than an advertised 75 bhp. Some versions had drum brakes all round, and almost all of them would have cross-ply tyres.

Hayes and Taylor brushed aside almost every

13

The pushrod-engined Escort Super of 1968, complete with rectangular headlamps. The Twin-Cam was saddled with these unsatisfactory components until mid-1969. Note that on the mass-production Escorts the suspension had 12-in wheels and cross-ply tyres

WWC 373F

practical difficulty. Both were now convinced that Ford needed a new 'homologation special' for 1968. To do that, they had to build prototypes very quickly, and the practical details could be tied up at a later date. Hayes duly went to his board, detailed the J25 scheme to them and came away with approval, at least for prototypes to be built.

But how to build—or even to convert—a prototype? The Escort, in the spring of 1967, was not yet even in pilot production, and no matter how much Henry Taylor and Walter Hayes begged at engineering, they would not release a representative running prototype. In the end, the engineers at the Dunton, Essex, engineering centre promised him a car—but it wasn't a runner and he couldn't have it for keeps. The best they could do was to *lend* him a plastic body-chassis unit over a weekend, to be returned, undamaged, by the following Tuesday.

To this day, Bill Meade has strong memories of what happened at Boreham:

'We stopped all normal work on a Friday afternoon in March when the "car" arrived on a truck. We shut the workshop doors, started there and then, and spent all weekend just mocking up a new car. . . . We worked to midnight on the Friday and probably 12-hour shifts on the Saturday and Sunday. . . . None of the drivers knew at that stage. I'm sure they were not told until we'd actually done the job. . . . It was all very rushed. We took a few measurements, but there were no drawings and not even any photographs for the record. . . . It would be three months before we could actually have a body to keep, and we could get the drawings done by then. . . .'

Most of the Escort's existing mechanical components—engine, gearbox, back axle and front suspension struts with brakes—were discarded, and the first 'look-see' concentrated on the

approximate fitting of the equivalent Lotus-Cortina or Capri items in their place.

Right away it became clear that there would be difficulties—not in terms of adding over-sophisticated components to a simple little body-shell, but of actually finding space for them. However, on the assumption that a slightly strengthened shell could be supplied from Hale-wood, and that a little judicious wielding of a big heavy hammer was justified, the axle, the more bulky gearbox, the front struts and brakes and even the bigger, wider 13-in wheels and tyres could be accommodated in the available space. It is true that wheel arch clearances were marginal, but that was as nothing compared with the problems in the engine bay. At first, quite literally, the engineers found themselves in a jam.

The Lotus-Ford twin-cam engine was not so

Eventually there would be two-door and four-door Escorts, but all RS models were based on the original two-door shell. This is an Escort 1100 De Luxe of 1968

'The office' of the 1968 Escort GT, showing off the instrument panel and seats which featured on original Twin-Cams which, effectively, were GTs with mechanical transplants

much high, as bulky. It was a very wide unit, not only because of the twin-cam cylinder head but because of the dual twin-choke Weber carburettors and their air cleaner. The first attempt to insert the engine was a disaster, for it fouled not only the wheel arches, but the battery, the clutch cable and the brake master cylinder. Something, quite clearly, would have to give.

The battery, at least, posed no lasting problem for, as with the Lotus-Cortina, it could be relocated in the boot (which would also help the weight distribution). The clutch and brake problem was solved very quickly by reverting to hydraulic clutch operation (which the Lotus-Cortina transmission had always had, in any case) and by relocating a new brake master cylinder and reservoir.

The major problem, however, was in finding clearance for the carburettors and their associated air-cleaner, which persistently fouled the offside panels in the engine bay, particularly the panel surrounding the suspension strut to the right-hand front wheel. The instant 'can-do' solution evolved at Boreham in that frantically busy weekend was one which no production-minded engineer would have entertained. Quite simply, the rear gearbox mounting position was retained, but because there was a lot more space now available on the left side of the engine bay (due to the removal of the battery and its tray to the boot), the nose of the engine was pushed across towards that side of the space.

It was a 'fix' which worked extraordinarily well. Although, in plan view, the engine was now positioned somewhat asymmetrically in the car (in other words, the crankshaft line was not truly fore-and-aft), it set up no unwanted vibrations, for the *overall* transmission line, from crankshaft to rear axle pinion, was straighter than usual.

On that first occasion, there was no question of making a car which could actually be driven. All that could be proved—albeit, rather provisionally—was that the desired parts could be fitted into a slightly-modified Escort bodyshell. The building of a true prototype would have to wait and for the moment Henry Taylor and Walter Hayes could only gloat, and rub their hands in anticipation. In 1967, their front-line competition car was the Mark II Lotus-Cortina, which weighed about 2000 lb, and could be tuned to produce 160 or 170 bhp. In 1968, if everything went well, they would be using a projectile weighing 150 lb less (nearly 10 per cent less) which could have as much, or even more, power.

It was an exciting prospect. They hoped—indeed, they were convinced—that the buying public would agree with them.

Chapter 2
The Twin-Cam years

Dick Boxall, whose job it was to find a simple way of producing Twin-Cams at Halewood, without disrupting the place completely

Once the mechanics at Boreham had proved that a Twin-Cam Escort *could* be made, and Walter Hayes had convinced his board that such cars *should* be made, the major debate began. To gain Group 2 homologation, facilities for building at least 1000 cars a year had to be found, and assembly line workers would be needed to screw them together. The obvious place to build the cars was at Halewood, where 'Job One' for the bread-and-butter Escorts was slated for November 1967: however, it was not at all certain that such heavily modified machines could be accommodated on lines used to making 1000 cars *a day* rather than 1000 cars a year.

For everyone who believed in the Twin-Cam— and that, really, was everyone at Ford with red blood in their veins—it was a difficult time. Production engineers at Halewood put forward reams of perfectly logical objections to such a car. It would need to have a different bodyshell, and they weren't sure they could cope with the necessary programming ... the engines would have to be dropped in from above, rather than slotted up from underneath ... the gearboxes wouldn't fit without a lot of heavy hammer work ... the axles were completely different, as were the front struts, and brakes. ... For a time, indeed, it looked as if the project might have to be cancelled. Dick Boxall, who was an executive at Halewood, was given an initial brief—he had to

find painless ways of building the first 200 Twin-Cams at Halewood in order to get the car well on its way, at least to Group 3 (500-off) homologation: greater quantities could then be considered in the light of his experiences.

There was no viable alternative, at that time, to building the cars at Halewood. For convenience's sake, therefore, it was agreed to make the Twin-Cam bodyshell (dubbed Type 49) a reinforced and slightly modified version of the Escort GT's two-door (Type 48) shell. All Escort bodies had type

The first Twin-Cam ever shown to the press—XTW 368F, with Bill Meade at the wheel, showing off its black grille and quarter bumpers. The Rostyle wheels were optional, never standard, and the 'speed stripes' were never fitted to production cars

21

The new-style Escorts were introduced to the press in driving sessions in Morocco, and the original Twin-Cam (it was the only complete running Twin-Cam at the time) was in great demand throughout

numbers, and I am assured that Types 48 and 49 were chosen by some romantic who realised that a Formula 2 Lotus-Ford was a Type 48 and a Formula 1 Lotus-Ford was a Type 49. . . .

The good news was that the Escort, even in standard form, had a very strong basic structure: to produce a Twin-Cam shell it was only necessary to arrange for local reinforcement of chassis rails, the floor pan and a few other details for changes to allow the more bulky Lotus-Cortina/Corsair 2000E type of gearbox to be fitted, and for slightly flared front and rear wheel arches to be provided to allow clearance for the larger 13-in wheels and 165-13-in radial ply tyres. It had been agreed in the meantime, that the Twin-Cam road cars would stay with the standard Escort GT rear damper positions and with the extra radius arms to locate the back axle. Proposals to fit a Panhard rod for extra transverse location were dropped at the prototype stage when prototype cars repeatedly broke the mounting brackets.

A minor but important front suspension geometry change was also accepted by Halewood's planners, because they already knew that they would be phasing it in for all other Escorts in the autumn of 1968. As originally designed, the Escort had a modified type of MacPherson strut front suspension, in which there was no anti-roll bar, and in which there was what was called a compression strut running back from the base of the suspension damper to the side rail. It didn't work very well, and in any case Boreham would have nothing to do with it. They plumped, right away, for the conventional MacPherson system which includes the use (on Fords) of a forward-mounted anti-roll bar which also doubles as a suspension link. The same layout, as I have already stated, was readopted for every other Escort within months.

The bad news, because interchangeability had to be maintained and because costs had to be kept in bounds, was the Escort GT trim and seats, along with the instruments, were part of the Twin-Cam's specification. Worse, for those enthusiasts who knew how bad they could be, the Twin-Cam was to be afflicted with the rectangular head-

The Twin-Cam in correct production form, with Lotus-Cortina steel wheels, Twin-Cam badges on the flanks, and without embellishment. You could have any colour you wanted as long as it was white. . . .

lamps which graced the more up-market pushrod engined Escorts.

The question of *where* to build the cars was, in the end, solved easily enough. Twin-Cams were to be built on the same production lines as the other Escorts, through body assembly, paint and trim areas, to a point at which the mechanical components were normally added. At this stage they would be whipped off the line, and taken into a separate, small, workshop where a dozen specially chosen (volunteer) workers were ready to slot in the unique components. After that each

Above *XOO 352F was one of the very first Twin-Cams, and was actually assembled at Boreham early in 1968. This was the car tested by Motor in April. The flared wheel arches are just visible in this view*

Left *The rear view of a Twin-Cam gives almost no clues to the special nature of the car. Only the wider-tread tyres and the larger-bore exhaust system are non-standard compared with pushrod models*

25

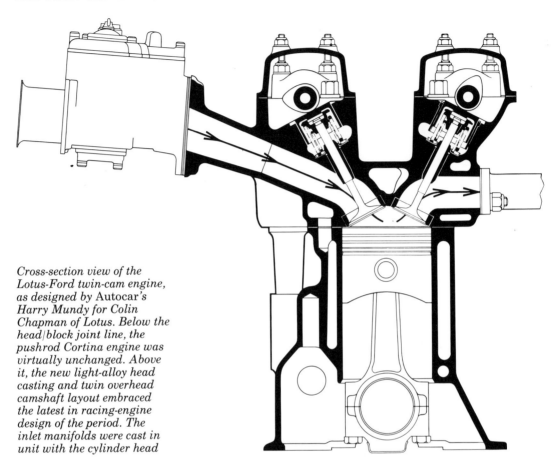

Cross-section view of the Lotus-Ford twin-cam engine, as designed by Autocar's Harry Mundy for Colin Chapman of Lotus. Below the head/block joint line, the pushrod Cortina engine was virtually unchanged. Above it, the new light-alloy head casting and twin overhead camshaft layout embraced the latest in racing-engine design of the period. The inlet manifolds were cast in unit with the cylinder head

Twin-Cam was treated to a road test of between 10 and 20 miles before it was shipped off to its purchaser.

When the Escort range was revealed to the public in January 1968, the Twin-Cam was not yet quite ready to go into quantity production for—even by Boreham's standards—nine months had not been long enough to complete the *productionising* of the design and to shake out the bugs. Unfortunately, the original prototype had been written off in early testing through a mechanical failure and the weather in the winter of 1967–68 was so bad that endurance work could not be completed ahead of time. Even so, the original car, given a new bodyshell after its big accident, not only completed a lot of destruction testing before the turn of the year, but was refurbished and sent out to Morocco for all the journalists to drive.

Some of us, a favoured few, had known since the previous autumn that a *very* exciting Escort was on the way. To others, the Twin-Cam came as an extremely pleasant surprise. Its price was not immediately revealed—for it was not then ready for sale—but when deliveries began many enthusiasts were astonished. Whereas a 1.3-litre Escort GT was priced at £794 (total), and the Mark II Lotus-Cortina cost £1123, the Twin-Cam was also priced at £1123—which meant that it was even better value-for-performance-for-money than previous 'go-faster' Fords.

For Ford, and for Henry Taylor, the problem was that they could not guarantee homologation before the spring, but they wanted to get cars to their customers. It was therefore decided that, somehow, the first 25 'production' (or—more truly—'pilot production') Twin-Cams would be assembled at Boreham, in the competitions department, and that for a few weeks at least all competitions activity would have to cease. It is now a matter of record that Group 3 homologation was achieved on 1 March 1968 and Group 2 homologation (which means that Ford convinced the authorities that the first 1000 cars had been completed) followed on 1 May 1968.

Roger Clark took a 'works' Twin-Cam (registered XOO 262F) to its first international victory in April, in the Circuit of Ireland rally, and followed that up a few days later by winning the Tulip Rally in another example. By the middle of the year Twin-Cams were winning in rallies *and* on the race track and it was already becoming

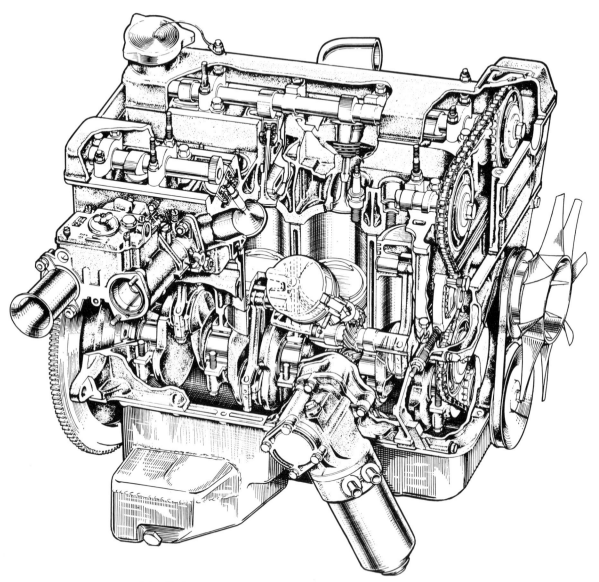

Above *Anatomy of the Twin-
Cam engine, laid bare.*
Right *An 'exploded' drawing
of the components used in the
twin overhead-camshaft
cylinder head of the Twin-
Cam*

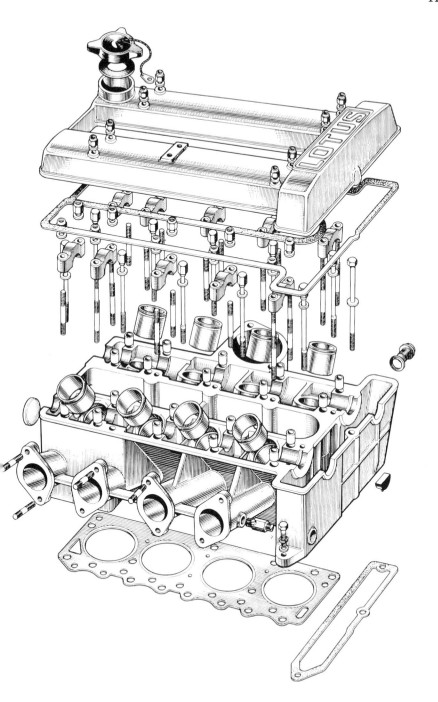

clear that all competitors would have to raise their sights and standards to catch up with them.

The competition successes, indeed, ran ahead of the publication of the magazine road tests of standard cars, so their performance was not at all unexpected when it was made public. As I have already said, the Twin-Cam was something like 150 lb lighter than a Lotus-Cortina, with which it shared the same 109.5 bhp (net) 1558 cc engine, built by Lotus at Hethel, near Norwich. It had the same gearbox, which was colloquially known as the '2000E' box after the Corsair model for which this item was originally developed, and even the same rear axle and axle ratio. It was no surprise, therefore, to see that a standard car could reach about 113 mph (at which point the Lucas distributor cut-out was actuated to limit engine speeds), that it could sprint to 60 mph in about 10 seconds, and to a quarter mile from rest in about 17 seconds, all at a typical fuel consumption (5-star, Super Premium grade) of about 24 to 25 mpg.

It was generally agreed that the Twin-Cam was a real 'hooligan's car' (*Autocar* thought it had 'startling performance . . .'), and that the handling was certainly very delicately balanced, with a tendency towards final oversteer, which made it a very nimble car for minor-road use. It was also pointed out that a Twin-Cam was not, and made no pretensions to be, a refined little car. Everyone seemed to realise that it was being sold as a basis for preparation for competition use, and that customers would take its hearty failings on face value.

And so they did. Queues built up and order books lengthened, well before the car was in anything like small-scale series production at Halewood. At first, something akin to a priority delivery system had to be set up, so that the most serious and deserving racing and rally teams, individuals, and dealers could get their cars as quickly as possible. Henry Taylor's deputy, Barrie Gill, found that one of his most important tasks in 1968 was to pacify angry customers who were having to wait for their cars to be scheduled and delivered.

One immediate effect of the Twin-Cam's popularity, incidentally, was that demand for the Mark II Lotus-Cortina (or the Cortina Twin-Cam, as it had officially become known from the end of 1967) took a tumble. Sales of this car, which was bigger, heavier, and altogether less nimble in character than the Escort Twin-Cam, never recovered as the orders from would-be competition users dried up completely. When the Mark II Cortina was dropped in 1970, the Lotus-Cortina concept disappeared, and has never been revived.

No one ever seemed to have doubts about buying such a special little car which was being built in a mass-production factory, and there were several reasons for this. As far as potential competition cars were concerned, the Twin-Cams, once delivered, were usually rushed into a workshop, stripped out and modified or re-prepared for a particular purpose. Another reason was that enthusiasts had realised just how bad a sports saloon could be, even when built by specialists, when they had bought the original Lotus-assembled Lotus-Cortinas; Ford, they reasoned, would surely be able to do better than that! Finally, of course, there was the fact that the Twin-Cam, as far as Halewood was concerned, was merely another assembly job to be completed efficiently, for none of the special items were actually manufactured 'on site'.

The most important component was, of course, the engine. This was manufactured and assembled by Lotus at Hethel, where some fine new tape-

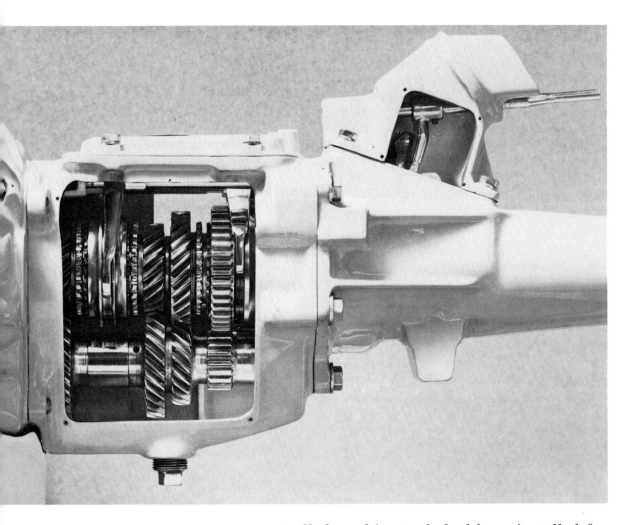

A demonstration model of the typical Ford gearbox of the day, from which the Twin-Cam box was developed. This example, in fact, is an earlier type with non-synchronised first gear

controlled machine tools had been installed for machining purposes. The cylinder blocks, which were modified versions of the Ford 'Kent' five-bearing 1499 cc items, came from Dagenham along with many other smaller components. The light-alloy cylinder heads were machined at Hethel too and complete engines were available for several purposes; some stayed at Hethel, for fitment to Lotus Elan and Elan Plus Two sports cars, some were sent to Dagenham for fitment to Mark II Lotus-Cortinas, and some went to Halewood for the Escort Twin-Cam. At the time, of course, the Twin-Cam engine was used extensively in competition cars—two-seater 'sports' types and single seaters—for several tuners had worked their particular type of magic on the basic Mundy-Chapman-Ford unit.

In standard form, the Twin-Cam's engine was rated at 109.5 bhp (net) at 6000 rpm, and to guard against over-revving (for standard connecting rods and a cast crankshaft were retained) there was a rev-limiting device built in to the Lucas distributor, nominally set to interrupt high-tension ignition supplies at 6500 rpm. This setting, incidentally, was somewhat variable— Ford's own road test car, as sampled by *Autocar* in June 1968, suffered cut-out at 6300 rpm. Some owners discarded the rev-limiter altogether (it was a very simple modification, involving a different rotor arm), over-revved their engines— and speedily discovered to their horror why one had been fitted in the first place!

The Twin-Cam's MacPherson strut front suspension, showing the forward-mounted anti-roll bar which also acted as a suspension link

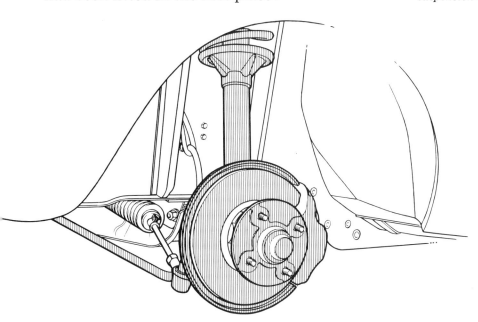

The versatile Ford back axle, used in Lotus-Cortina, Corsair 2000E and Twin-Cam alike. For Twin-Cam use, there was also radius-arm location, and the lugs for this do not appear on this Corsair axle

The Twin-Cam's engine was, to all intents and purposes, identical with that fitted to the Mark II Lotus-Cortina, even to the extent of using the same carburettor settings, the same air box and air cleaner (which was mounted, askew, on top of the camshaft covers). Extra-powerful versions were fitted to some of the Lotus sports cars, and it was very easy for any Twin-Cam owner to shop around for tune-up kits to make his own car's engine even more lusty than it was in 'as-delivered' condition.

The standard dimensions were 82.55 × 72.8 mm bore and stroke, with a capacity of 1558 cc. The fitment of only marginally oversize pistons allowed the engine to be enlarged to the competition class limit of 1600 cc. Where no such class limitations applied, and with the aid of specially selected thick-wall cylinder blocks, it was possible to bore the engine out to about 1800 cc, though there was no question of any guarantees of reliability being available after that sort of treatment. The works rally cars had engines producing more than 155/160 bhp at 7500 rpm (which not only involved the use of different camshaft profiles and re-worked cylinder heads but also made the use of special steel crankshaft and rods absolutely essential), and 'sprint' racing engines with fuel-injection could be persuaded to produce up to 180 bhp.

Lotus's production experience since 1962 had allowed what had once been an unreliable and temperamental 'conversion' to become a lusty and flexible quantity-production unit. It says much for its design that well over 25,000 such engines, of all types, were eventually built before Lotus discontinued manufacture in favour of their own more modern four-valve-per-cylinder 'slant' four-

Twin-Cam rear suspension included twin radius-arm location, above the line of the half-elliptic leaf springs

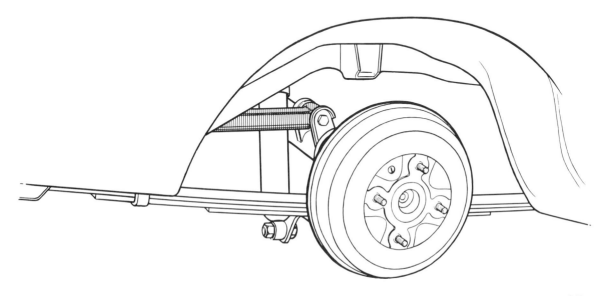

cylinder unit. Harry Mundy, the designer who made it all possible, has lamented since then that he turned down Colin Chapman's offer of a £1 royalty on every engine built in favour of a lump sum payment for the work he did!

The Twin-Cam's gearbox was pure Ford of the type used in the Lotus-Cortina, the Corsair 2000E and the Cortina 1600E and had synchromesh on all forward speeds, an excellent remote control gearchange, and was driven through an 8-in Borg and Beck diaphragm spring clutch. Such gearboxes, incidentally, were manufactured in a transmissions factory also at Halewood, but in a building entirely separate from the main motor car assembly facilities. For competition use, alternative close-ratio gear sets were available, and from 1970 it was even possible to substitute a more massive five-speed ZF gearbox, though such sophisticated fittings were never made available on production-line cars.

The back axle and brakes were pure Lotus-Cortina/Corsair/Cortina GT—the axle being manufactured at a Ford factory in Swansea—while the front brakes, 9.62-in discs, were shared with the high-performance Cortinas and the suspension strut settings were special to the Twin-Cam. The road wheels and tyres—165-13-in radials, on 5.5-in rims—were also those of the Lotus-Cortina, but the sculptured Rostyle wheels of the Cortina 1600E could also be fitted at extra cost.

Apart from the wheels and tyres themselves, and the fact that the Twin-Cam sat rather lower to the ground than did normal Escorts, the only way to recognise a Twin-Cam externally was really by looking at its badges (one on each front wing, above and behind the wheel arches and one on the boot lid), and then by noting the black-painted grille. Inside the car, it all looked like the interior

of an Escort GT except for the marking of the instruments (even the rather nasty three-spoke mass-production Escort steering wheel was retained), though a look in the boot revealed a battery to one side of the floor, and the wide-rimmed spare wheel bolted to the floor itself. A look underneath would have revealed the use of

Roger Clark and Jim Porter, on their way to the Twin-Cam's first rallying success, in the 1968 Circuit of Ireland rally

37

One of the last Twin-Cams, registered in 1970, with non-standard Minilite wheels, and with the later round-headlamp nose

twin radius arms for axle location, in exactly the same way as the Escort GT fittings. Incidentally, although four-door versions of all other Escorts were made available from the autumn of 1969, no four-door Twin-Cam was ever made available.

The only development change of note—and one which came as a tremendous relief to every

38

customer who used his Twin-Cam for rallying at night—was that the original rectangular headlamp arrangement was discarded in July 1969 in favour of the circular headlamp installation of the other so-called 'cheaper' Escorts. Up until this point, incidentally, Boreham had been forced to co-operate with Cibié in concocting a lash-up involving circular lenses behind rectangular clear-glass or Perspex covers in an only partly successful attempt to improve the lighting performance of these cars. It was a particularly stubborn piece of product planning which had inflicted such poor lamps on a car with a 115 mph performance.

Several minor changes, connected with the trim and equipment of Twin-Cams, were made from time to time, but this was only to keep the cars abreast of the modifications being applied to mass-production Escorts. It would be fair to say, indeed, that once the minimum numbers of cars had been built to satisfy the sporting authorities and allow the car to be used in Group 2 (rallying) or Group 5 (racing) events, the factory rather lost interest in the Twin-Cam, as it was rather a difficult car properly to 'package' for the general public, and it was a car many Ford dealers did not even try to understand, or to sell.

By the end of 1969, less than two years after the Twin-Cam had been announced, it had already become outclassed as a rally car and greater and even more exciting projects were under way behind closed doors. Walter Hayes and Stuart Turner had put their heads together once again— this time in conjunction with the redoubtable Keith Duckworth of Cosworth—to evolve an even more remarkable engine. Eight-valve Lotus power was about to be overwhelmed by 16-valve Cosworth power—the BDA engine, and the RS1600, were on their way.

Chapter 3
Twin-Cam plus
BDA=RS1600

Stuart Turner, Ford's competitions chief from 1969, who got together with Keith Duckworth to devise a way of using the new BDA engine in the Escort

The story of Ford's famous 16-valve BDA engine, which powered the RS1600 and—later—the RS1800 road cars and a host of successful competition cars, really starts with Colin Chapman in 1965 and with his desperate search for a new 3-litre Grand Prix engine. The connection is rather tenuous, the sequence of events being given below.

By 1963—64, Coventry Climax racing engines were supreme in Grand Prix racing, so that when it was announced that a new 3-litre formula would become effective in 1966, it was generally assumed that Coventry Climax would build a new engine to suit. When they announced, at the beginning of 1965, that they would *not* be doing so, the other constructors started looking around for alternatives. Colin Chapman tried several schemes, and approached several other concerns, before getting together with Walter Hayes during the summer of 1965.

Chapman and Hayes eventually agreed that Ford ought to get together with Keith Duckworth, the founder and design genius of Cosworth Engineering, in a scheme whereby Duckworth would first design a 1.6-litre Formula 2 engine based on a Ford Cortina cylinder block, and then would go ahead on the design of a completely special V8 3-litre Grand Prix engine. The four-cylinder F2 design would be made public in 1966, and the V8 was to be ready by the spring of 1967.

History now shows that this scheme, which initially cost Ford the paltry sum of £100,000, was a resounding success, for both engines were amazingly successful right from the start. However, even before the V8 engine appeared and while the four-cylinder FVA was winning its first races, Walter Hayes was thinking ahead. Well before the end of the year he, in conjunction with Henry Taylor, had approached Duckworth again, and asked him to incorporate all the knowledge of four-valves-per-cylinder engineering gained on the pure racing engines into a new design—one which could be used in future Ford road cars. Thus it was that the experience of the FVA (four-cylinder) and DFV (V8 cylinder) engines came to be used in a new design—the BDA.

It is worth pointing out, right away, that the BDA engine is *not* a productionised version of the FVA, and that therefore it is quite untrue to suggest that the RS1600 and RS1800 road cars were equipped with de-tuned racing engines. The fact that Hayes and Taylor always visualised the new design as being as ultimately tunable is quite another story altogether. . . .

The original Formula 2 FVA engine was a Cosworth conversion of a non-cross flow 1499 cc Cortina engine, with its twin overhead camshafts driven by a train of gears, and with a bore and stroke of 85.7 × 69.3 mm, which brought its capacity up to 1599 cc. The new engine which Duckworth was asked to design, the BDA, was a Cosworth conversion of a crossflow 1599 cc Cortina engine, which had an entirely different and deeper cylinder block; had its twin overhead camshafts driven by a reinforced cogged rubber belt, and retained the original pushrod engine's bore and stroke of 80.97 × 77.62 mm, 1599 cc. The

Keith Duckworth—the engine designing genius (no less forceful word will accurately describe his talents) who produced the four-cylinder FVA, the V8 Grand Prix DFV, and the productionised BDA, all within three years

41

basic layout of the four-valves-per-cylinder cylinder head was carried over, but the castings, the mode of valve operation, and all the details were completely different. Because the new engine used the deeper cylinder block, the FVA's gear drive (even if suitable for road use, which it wasn't, because of the noise it created) would not have fitted into place.

Ford's own cutaway drawing of the BDA engine in production form, showing the 16-valve layout, and the belt-drive to the camshafts

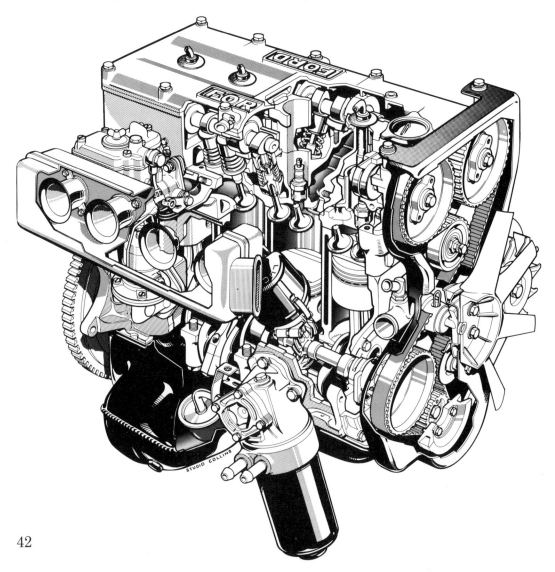

FVA and BDA? What on earth did they mean? They were both engine codes invented by the ruthlessly logical and definitely unromantic Keith Duckworth—FVA stood for Four Valves, Series A, while BDA stood for Belt Drive, Series A. Duckworth's approach to engine titles began years earlier when he started preparing Ford Anglia engines for racing; he gave them the title of MAE, which means, no more and no less, Modified Anglia Engine!

Duckworth's brief regarding a 16-valve engine for road cars was to retain as much of the standard 1.6-litre Cortina engine as possible. At first, with the exception of the crankshaft and the timing gear, the bottom half of the engine including the pistons and connecting rods, was exactly the same as that of the Cortina GT model, with an unmodified 1599 cc *cast-iron* cylinder block being used. However, whereas for the Lotus engine of 1962 Harry Mundy had chosen to specify two valves per cylinder, opposed symmetrically at an included angle of 54 degrees, in a part-spherical combustion chamber, Keith Duckworth's plan for the new BDA was to have four valves per cylinder—two inlet and two exhaust—opposed at an included angle of 40 degrees in a pent-roof combustion chamber. Both engines, incidentally, accurately reflected mainstream racing engine design thinking at the time.

Although Keith Duckworth was careful to make sure that a race-tuned BDA engine would be competitive, his road-car derivative was quite severely de-tuned. With mild valve timing, and two horizontal twin-choke Weber Carburettors, its peak power output was 120 bhp (DIN) at 6500 rpm, and the peak of the very broad-shouldered torque curve was at 112 lb ft at 4000 rpm. Indeed, it was such an efficient little engine at first that it looked as if it could be run on 2-star fuel! The early road

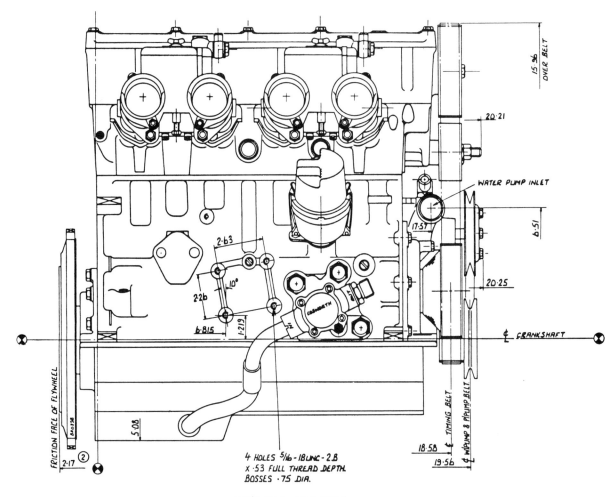

RIGHT HAND SIDE VIEW.

Dimensional side view of the production-based BDB, and . . .

test cars could certainly use this cheap fuel without protest, which is quite remarkable when the 10:1 compression ratio is considered.

The prototype engines ran in 1968 and the design was revealed, somewhat prematurely, in January 1969 at the same time as Ford showed off their new 2+2 Capri coupés. At the time, it was suggested, no definite decisions had been taken

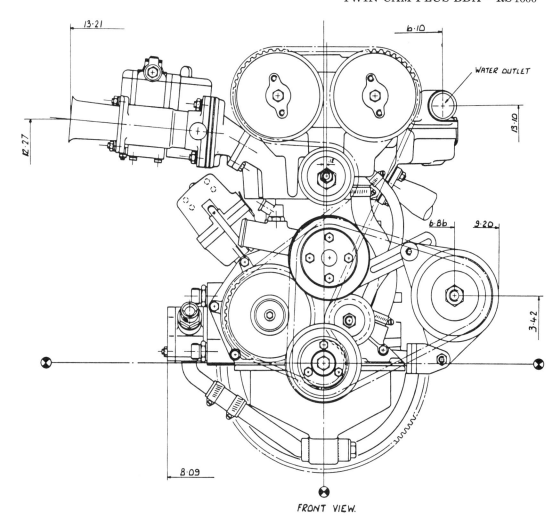

FRONT VIEW.

... the front view of the same engine, in dry-sump guise

about the BDA's future, except that 100 'Twin-Cam Capris' would eventually be built in a limited series. This was no more than kite-flying, to assess public interest and, in the event, no BDA-engined Capris were ever sold to the public.

The BDA engine then disappeared from public view and at one time Keith Duckworth thought that it was going to be dropped altogether. It was

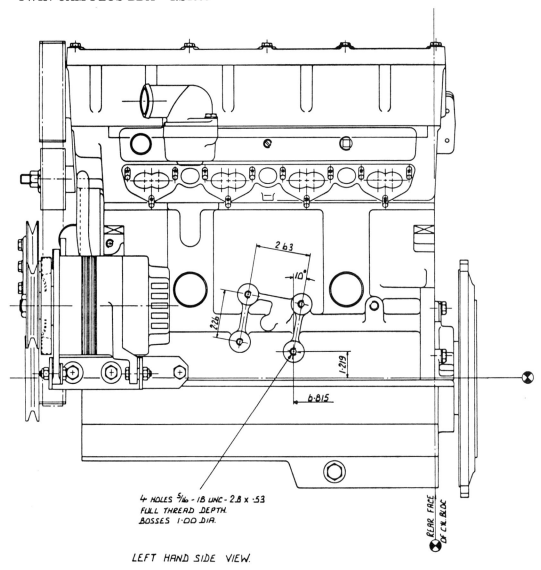

4 HOLES 5/16 - 18 UNC - 2B x ·53
FULL THREAD DEPTH.
BOSSES 1·00 DIA.

LEFT HAND SIDE VIEW.

The left side (exhaust side) view, showing the siamesed exhaust ports of the BDA. This is a dry-sumped BDB derivative

not until Stuart Turner joined Ford in June 1969—and soon discovered that he would need more power for his rallying Escorts if they were to continue to be rally winners—that interest was rekindled. The author is still proud of the fact that it was he who actually introduced Turner

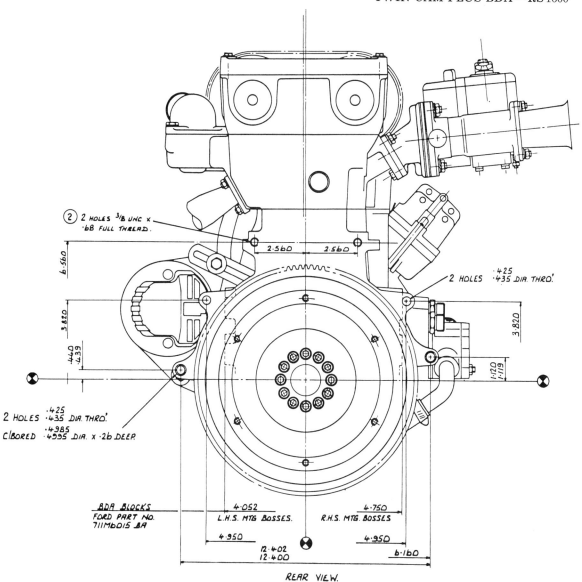

REAR VIEW.

and Duckworth to each other at a private dinner party in the Midlands, and it was on that occasion that the proposed marriage of the BDA engine with the Escort motor car was discussed.

In the meantime, Ford's interest in the build-ing and merchandising of special cars and ac-

The rear drawing of the BDB, complete with external oil pump and piping

47

A display version of the 16-valve, 1.6-litre BDA engine, as used in the RS1600

cessories had continued to expand. Sales of special parts from Boreham exceeded £50,000 in 1968 and looked likely to pass the £250,000 mark in 1970. At the same time, Ford's interest in promoting the sporting fellowship among their owners had become crystallised in the Rallye Sport Club. From here, it was only a short step for Walter Hayes to dream up the idea of setting up a special network for selling the more specialised Fords, and even to look around for a small facility where such special cars could be built.

At the beginning of 1970, therefore, Ford made an important announcement. Not only, they said, were they about to begin selling a new breed of Escort—the BDA-engined RS1600—but they proposed to do this through a new organisation to be known as the Ford Advanced Vehicle Operation and through a limited number of specially-selected dealers. For the moment, however, it was clear that the RS1600 would have to be built at

Above *The early RS1600s of 1970 were virtually indistinguishable from the Twin-Cams apart from their new badges*

Left *The BDA cylinder head, valve gear and inlet manifolds; the four-valves per cylinder layout is obvious*

49

Above *The Soderstrom-Palm 'works' Twin-Cam in the 1968 Alpine Rally*

Above Right *The RS1600 in production form*

Near Right *Stuart McCrudden demonstrating the handling properties of the RS1600*

Far Right *RS=Rallye Sport, or is short for RS1600 on cars of that type*

Halewood, in harness with the Twin-Cam, as the special assembly factory site had not been revealed, and would not be ready for use until the late autumn.

Although, in sporting terms, there was nothing particularly new about 16-valve Escorts (a Cosworth FVA-engined rally car had been used in practice for the 1968 French Alpine Rally), getting the BDA-engined car into production took time. Ford had no intention of manufacturing the engines themselves, Cosworth were not equipped to tackle series-production build and for political reasons Lotus could not be invited to do so. After a long search, however, a production contract for the machining and assembly of BDA engines, went to Harpers of Letchworth.

RS1600 on the front wings, and an RS badge on the boot lid tell us that this Escort has the BDA engine installed

The first Halewood-built RS1600s were not available until May 1970, though Roger Clark notched up the first 'works' rally car success in the Circuit of Ireland in March, when he won the event outright in a 'prototype' car converted from one of the new Monte Carlo Rally Twin-Cams.

The difference between Twin-Cam and RS1600 road cars was almost entirely confined to the engine, for body styling, general equipment, transmission, suspension settings and brakes were all unchanged. It was a very simple change for the specially-selected Halewood workforce to learn, as they had to do no more than fit a different shape of special engine, in the way to which they had become accustomed since early 1968.

Above Left *The RS1600 instrument panel was based on that of the Twin-Cam, and therefore of the Escort GT*

Above Right *The interior of the RS1600 road car was very basic—most owners soon installed special seats for competition use*

Spotting the differences, externally, was difficult, for these were confined to new wheel arch and boot lid badges stating 'RS1600' instead of 'Twin-Cam'. As before, you could have any colour you liked, as long as it was white, with black interior trim. Neither was there much difference in performance, for the RS1600, like the Twin-Cam, was fitted with an electrical rev-limiter. *Autocar*'s test car—a pre-production example—reached a top speed of 113 mph (with the rev-limiter cutting in at 6300 rpm), got to the quarter mile mark in 16.7 seconds, and recorded overall fuel consumption of 21.5 mpg. The extra 10 bhp of the 16-valve engine, and the more flexible torque characteristics, helped to give a little extra

A rather travel-stained RS1600, showing the later type of air cleaner, and the bracketry for extra lamps which AVO could supply

acceleration, but on the open road it is doubtful if many customers noticed this.

If, however, the RS1600 had more tuning potential, it was also more expensive. By the spring of 1970 the price of a Twin-Cam had risen to £989 (basic—in Britain the total cost was £1291), but the RS1600 was ushered in at £1108 basic, £1447 total; almost penny for penny the same as a Triumph TR6! In the 1980s, both these prices look absurdly cheap, but in 1970 terms this made the RS1600 a rather expensive luxury—and it was, of course, 12 per cent more costly than the Twin-Cam. Not that this deterred the queues from forming and, just as the Twin-Cam had killed demand for the Lotus-Cortina, so did the RS1600 strike a mortal blow at the Escort Twin-Cam. Although the two cars were similar, yet different, the RS1600 was both more sophisticated and potentially much more powerful. Although the Twin-Cam was not dropped (it remained on the market, in fact, until the summer of 1971), it fell out of the limelight almost at once.

For use in international competitions however, the Twin-Cam still had its uses, for RS1600 homologation was not achieved until October 1970. The Twin-Cam's last works team entry, incidentally, was in the East African Safari of April 1971, where all the team cars found themselves outpaced (although they managed fourth and sixth places), which made an immediate conversion to RS1600s imperative.

Although this is not a book which is primarily concerned with Escorts in competition use, it is important that I should now make the RS1600's homologation details clear. Whereas the Twin-Cam had been homologated at 1558 cc (which it was) and could only be used in the up-to-1600 cc class, the RS1600 was homologated at 1601 cc!

According to the nominal dimensions, the BDA engine, like the Cortina/Capri 1.6-litre unit on which it was based, had a cylinder bore of 80.97 mm and a stroke of 77.62 mm. This, carefully calculated, gives a swept volume of 1598.7 cc,

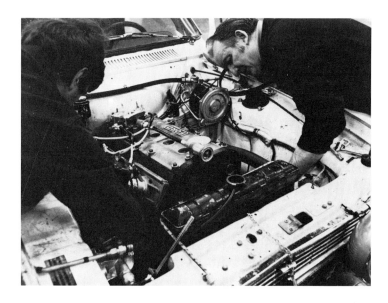

Installing a fuel-injected 2-litre BDA in a 'works' rally car at Boreham in 1972. Roger Clark used such an engine to win the RAC Rally of that year

which falls neatly under the 1.6-litre sporting class limit. Stuart Turner, however, knew that the engine could safely be enlarged to 1.8-litres, and decided that the car should be homologated as an *over* 1600 cc car. Since it was (and still is) a fact that production tolerances of bore and stroke dimensions could allow the capacity to differ between about 1596 cc and 1603 cc, it was decided to quote the stroke at a nominal 77.72 mm (an increase of 0.1 mm, or a mere four thousandths of an inch) when the swept volume most obligingly became 1601 cc. I should emphasise, however, that in its nominal internal dimensions the RS1600 (and the Mexico of 1970–74, for that matter) was never different in any way from the pushrod engines on which it was based.

The RS1600 model was to remain in production for nearly five years, and was homologated into FIA Group 2 (1000 examples built in less than 12 consecutive months) in October 1970, and although exact production figures are not available from Ford it seems that production during that period exceeded the number of Twin-Cams turned out between 1968 and 1971. However, quite a number of ageing Twin-Cams were converted into RS1600s by their owners (the conversion is relatively simple, if not cheap), and the only way in which this could be detected is by studying the vehicle's chassis number. (In the case of a conversion done for dishonest purposes, even that might have been changed!)

The introduction of the RS1600 was only the start of the marketing revolution being planned by Ford. Even while the first cars were being delivered, the new factory (always unofficially known as 'AVO') was being prepared. The Rallye Sport operation has a pivotal influence on the whole of this story, and its development must now be analysed.

Chapter 4
AVO—Car building in miniature

The decision to establish a small, separate, production facility for sporting Escorts was taken in January 1970, but the *idea* had been floating around in the Ford corporate mind for at least two years before that. In that month, however, Ray Horrocks was appointed 'Manager—AVO, Ford of Europe', with a devastating but demanding brief: 'to set up a self-contained organisation, formed exclusively to co-ordinate the development, assembly and sale of unique volume derivatives of the European product range, and associated parts and accessories'—orders which he had framed, and hung on the wall behind his desk.

The Advanced Vehicle Operation (which, henceforth, I will merely call by its initials) *was* Horrocks at first, until he could appoint his key staff members, and for a time his assembly facilities were no more than an empty 85,000 sq ft complex of buildings at South Ockendon in Essex, part of which had once been used by Ford's design and development staff and some of which—more recently—had been part of the Spares Division. Even before the assembly line took shape, the Rallye Sport dealers had to be appointed—originally there were 65 of them, spread as far apart as Perth and St Austell, Belfast and Brighton.

Ray Horrocks, later to become chairman of BL Cars, was the original manager of the Ford Advanced Vehicle Operation factory when it opened at South Ockendon in 1970

57

The 'merry-go-round'
assembly line for Escort RS
models at South Ockendon,
active from 1970 to 1974

The intention was that Escort bodyshells—painted, trimmed and with vital plumbing and wiring installations already in place—would be delivered to AVO from Halewood, after which assembly of all the special components into the car would be completed and the cars would then be delivered. This arrangement and the plan that more intensive development of further special cars would take place, meant that the 'hottest' Escorts would not find their specification completely constrained by the practical limitations of a large mass-production assembly plant.

Ford's initial public announcements mentioned a total workforce of 300 people, an ability to assemble up to 2750 cars in 1971, the first full year, and future expansion of up to 6000 cars a year. The first 500 RS1600s, it was stated, would be built at Halewood, after which assembly would begin at AVO in November 1970. The Twin-Cam, however, was to continue (and to end its days) at Halewood. It was not spelt out at the time, but always tacitly made clear, that the RS1600 would not, by any means, be the only model to be built at the new plant.

The heart of the plant was a 'merry-go-round' assembly line, the type where massive slings which support the painted and trimmed bodyshell while the mechanical items are fitted from below, at ground level hang from an overhead conveyor.

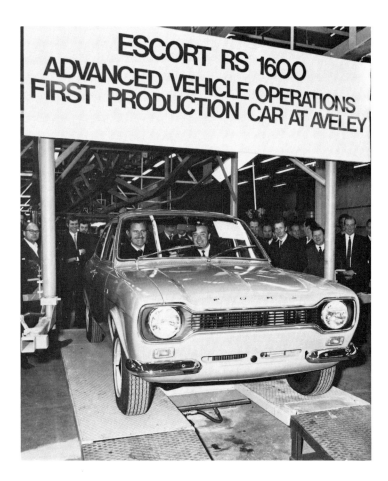

Story without words—the driver is Graham Hill, the passenger Ray Horrocks, the location South Ockendon in the autumn of 1970

Above *Offering up a push-rod Mexico engine to the cradle already supporting the cross-member of such a model*

Right *Hannu Mikkola and Gunnar Palm won the 1970 Daily Mirror World Cup Rally in what was really a pushrod-engined RS1600. It was from this win that the series-production 'Mexico' got its name*

Bodies join the merry-go-round just after completed cars have dropped off it, and at normal speeds a car takes a full day to make the single circuit and to complete assembly. In addition, there were paint facilities (to rectify any flaws inflicted on the way down M6 and M1 from Halewood by transporter), rolling-road brake dynamometers to check power outputs 'off-line' water test facilities and space to allow special equipment to be added, before or after the normal assembly process had been completed.

Preparation work was complete by the end of October 1970 and the very first AVO-built car (or so it says on the factory-supplied caption) was driven off the merry-go-round on 2 November 1970 by Graham Hill, with a grinning Ray Horrocks

Right *A typical Ford dealer display, to remind customers where the 'Mexico' name came from*

Below *Peter Ashcroft was Boreham's engine-development specialist in 1970, when the World Cup Rally was won, became competitions manager under Stuart Turner in 1972, and now manages the entire Ford Europe competitions activities in 1981*

sitting alongside him; it was a white RS1600 with right-hand drive, destined for a British customer.

By this time, however, it was no longer a secret that Ford were about to add a pushrod-engined Escort to the Rallye Sport range. The excuse was that, in April and May 1970, they had dominated the *Daily Mirror*'s London–Mexico World Cup Rally with a team of 1835 cc pushrod-engined Escorts (these engines, developed by Peter Ashcroft at Boreham, had non-standard dimensions of 85 mm bore and 80.8 mm stroke and produced about 140 bhp) and so they were preparing to sell de-tuned—and much more standard, mechanically—replicas. The cars when they were

made public later in November 1970, were indeed called Mexicos, but I suspect that the project had been under way for some time before the World Cup Rally was won.

Although the Mexico was not strictly an 'RS' Escort (it had, after all, an absolutely untuned 1.6-litre Cortina GT/Capri GT engine) it was always built in the AVO factory, and it was the derivative of which most examples were built, so it must be mentioned here. Rather than being an up-engined ordinary Escort, incidentally, it was more of a de-tuned RS1600, for it retained the reinforced bodyshell, the gearbox, axle, brakes, suspension and instrumentation of that car. Only

The Escort Mexico in all its striped glory, complete with 1600GT badges. The body shell, suspension and brakes were all exactly those of the RS1600, but the engine was a pushrod 'Kent' unit

Above *An RS1600 and a Mexico posed at Brands Hatch with a BDA-engined single seater and (in the background) a Kent-engined Formula Ford car*

Right *John Fitzpatrick used to race this RS1600 with suitable (false!) numberplates, for Broadspeed in 1971. It was quite capable of outright victory over much larger and more powerful opposition*

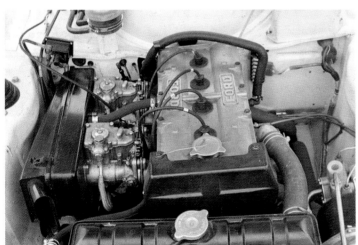

Above *Ford's archive tells us these are Twin-Cams at Oulton Park in 1970. There is no visual difference between the Twin-Cam and the RS1600, except for the side and boot-lid badges. In fact, the registration numbers suggest these are RS1600s . . .*

Left *The Ford-Cosworth BDA engine, as installed in the RS1600, showing that it was mounted askew to provide clearance between the big Weber carburettors and the air cleaner, and the inner wheel arch*

Above *Six Escort RS models
on a Ford Transporter—
about two hours' production
from the South Ockendon
plant. Three are Mexicos
with stripes and 1600GT
badges, one is an unadorned
Mexico, but with 'Mexico'
badging, while the other two
are RS1600s—one of which
has extra rallying lamps
already fitted*

Right *As so often seen, a
1971 Mexico, complete with
its colour-contrasting stripes.
On this car the cast-alloy
Minilite wheels and the row
of auxiliary rally lamps have
been fitted after initial
assembly at South Ockendon*

Left *One of the very exclusive Mexico Estate cars, fitted with the optional RS road wheels*
Above *Left to right, an RS1600 on Minilite wheels, an RS2000 Mk I with four extra lamps, an RS2000 Mk I, and an RS1600 with RS cast-alloy road wheels*
Right *A Ford Motor Co. studio shot of the first-ever RS1800, showing the horizontal two-tone blue colour stripe, the '1.8' badges behind the front wheel cut outs, and the RS1800 transfers on the rear quarter just ahead of the tan tamp clusters. A road-going RS1800 was a very rare bird indeed . . .*

Series X Escort

You specify as much or as little as you like

With Series X kits you can add authentic Rallye Sport style and performance to your Escort. You can specify more power, bigger brakes, stiffer suspension, lightweight alloy wheels, airdam, spoiler, wheel arches — with Series X you make as much or as little change as you like

Nothing could be more flexible. Be an individual, go Series X!

The Escort illustrated is fitted with the following combination of Series X parts:

**Rally specification wing extensions, front and rear spoiler together with 6 x 13"
RS alloy wheels and 185/70 tyres
Two fully reclining seats with head restraints
Gas-filled suspension with increased capacity springs
Limited slip differential**

ESCORT

*Left One of Ford's 'Series X'
adverts of 1979 and 1980. The
car used is one of the
homologated flat-nose
RS2000s (although such a
car was never built in series
in West Germany), complete
with RS wheels, rally-type
wheel arch extensions, and
bonnet retaining pins*

Above *It was possible to spend a great deal of money in 'X-Pack' equipment on a late-model RS2000. Visible here are the Zakspeed-style 'racing' wheel arch extensions at front and rear, the extra large 'chin' spoiler complete with brake cooling ducts, the very wide RS-style polished alloy wheels and matching tyres, and the special bonnet catches*

Above *Facing the camera is a 1979 RS2000 'Custom', while a 1978 RS2000 turns its spoilered boot lid to the world*

Right *The best-selling Escort RS model of all was the wedge-nosed RS2000 of 1976–1980. This was a 1979 'Custom' model, and it has a non-standard sun roof fitted*

the 'Kent' engine, an 86 bhp unit, had been changed.

For the same reason as for the RS1600, the Mexico, when homologated for sporting purposes in May 1972, was quoted as having an engine capacity of 1601 cc, which explains why it was never truly competitive in races or rallies: it was most normally used in strictly-standard 'Group 1' guise. Like all other Escorts ever assembled at the AVO factory, it had only two passenger doors. However it was from this time that the Mexico, and the RS1600 cars, both became available in a variety of colours instead of in the mandatory white. Normally a Mexico was also equipped with 'go-faster' stripes along its flanks and across the boot lid, but these could be omitted when the car was newly built if the customer specified this on his order. Otherwise, the only Mexico identification was by the badges on the front wings, and on the boot lid. In the grille/headlamp layout,

A 'Special Build' RS1600 from AVO, showing the flared wheel arches, the Minilite wheels, and the four extra driving lamps, all of which could be added to the car before it was even delivered to the dealer

Some of the extra fittings which could be added to a new AVO-built Mexico or RS1600 before it was delivered to the customer. This was called the 'Clubman Pack' and was suitable for rally cars

decoration, and in the layout of instrumentation the Mexico was the same as the RS1600.

Clearly, Ford were likely to sell many more Mexicos than RS1600s, even though it was a much slower car. (Road tests credited the Mexico with a maximum speed of around 100 mph, 0–60 mph acceleration in about 13 seconds, a standing-start quarter mile in 18 seconds, and overall fuel consumption of 27 to 28 mpg.) For those who needed it, the engine was very tunable, and for those who did not, it was still adequately quick, and possessed of the same responsive handling that the Twin-Cams and RS1600s had always had. It was a much cheaper car than either of the other special Escorts, and this, together with its simpler

mechanical specification, made it a much easier car to afford, and to insure. When launched in November 1970 a Mexico cost £1150 (total), at a time when the last of the Twin-Cams sold for £1360 and the hard-to-get RS1600s sold for £1447. No wonder that Ford let it be known that they were already equipped to build at least 5000 Mexicos every year and that they expected to sell every one without much difficulty.

In the meantime the RS1600, complete with its 16-valve Cosworth-designed engine, took most of the publicity and was naturally the choice for racing and rallying. It helped a lot, in 1971, that Broadspeed set John Fitzpatrick to racing a 'works-assisted' example, and—for track use

By the early 1970s, the number of homologated options for Mexicos and RS1600s was seemingly endless, as this studio shot makes clear. In this case, everything on show is for the Kent-engined Mexico

75

only—gave it the purely fictitious registration number of . . . RS1600. (In fact, it should have been MEV 34J, but we won't quibble about that.)

It would be quite impossible to list all the minor development changes made to the RS1600 during its life, as these were phased in, without drama, whenever, such modifications were made to the bread-and-butter Escorts. A slightly more

The smouldering 'Man about Town' is actually Allan Wilkinson, an AVO development engineer at the time, later to achieve more fame as Boreham's Rally Engineer man at a time when the RS1800s were becoming dominant in World Championship rallying. The car is a Mexico, built in 1973 with flared arches and non-standard wheels and tyres

Ford Escort Mexico.

Who says there's no room for the individual?

ergonomic instrument panel was standardised from the start of the 1971 model year, and trim and furnishing received regular but minor attention. The optional extra equipment available, however, continued to burgeon, mostly from Boreham where an aggressive development programme always seemed to be in progress to make the car stronger and faster. If it wasn't an 1800 cc engine it was a five-speed gearbox: if it wasn't four-wheel disc brakes it was a coil sprung back axle. There were wheel arch extensions, dry sump kits, oil cooler kits, different wheels, dampers, exhaust systems, clutches, seats . . . along with roll-cages, auxiliary lamp fittings, electronic ignition, and more—much, much more.

It was to satisfy what was clearly a big demand for ultra-special RS Escorts that AVO's activities were expanded in the spring of 1972. At this time it was stated that they were not only willing to supply their already-available 'Clubman' pack (Bilstein dampers, roll-cage, competition seats and auxiliary lamps—£138), but that they would now supply any or all of up to 100 special items under their new Special Build programme, so that it was possible 'to order an RS1600 or a Mexico to full international race or rally specification'. Rod Mansfield and Bill Meade found themselves in charge of a very specialised little corner of the works where new cars were turned out to sell for well over double the AVO production line cost. A 'standard' RS1600 cost £1495 in early 1971, yet a Special Build machine might easily set back its new owner more than £3000 or—if he had any engine work done—£4000. Modified engines, however, were not available officially, and most customers were advised to see to this themselves after the car was delivered. At a time when one normally had to wait more than a month for a standard RS model,

Rod Mansfield not only sold Escort RS Models from the AVO facility, but he also found time to race Twin-Cams and Mexicos with some success

'Special Build' AVO Mexicos, being prepared for a winter rally in the early 1970s. These were not *factory rally cars*

the attentions of Special Build usually added another eight or nine weeks to the delay.

In the meantime, one sensational development for the RS1600 was brewing. It had been clear for some time that the engines fitted with standard cylinder blocks could not safely and predictably be enlarged very far, and that even those special blocks with siamesed cylinder bores (colloquially known at Ford as the 'Ashcroft' block—for it was Peter Ashcroft who first persuaded the foundry engineers to make such modifications for his use) were really good for no more than about 1.8-litres. To solve this—entirely for his own purposes, and as a private venture—engine tuner-builder Brian Hart of Harlow New Town, designed and had built a new cylinder block, in which the casting profiles were so altered that it was just possible to bore out the cylinder walls to give a capacity of nearly

2 litres. To be precise, the standard cylinder bore was 80.97 mm, the safe limit of enlargement with the 'Ashcroft' block was about 86 mm, but with the new 'Brian Hart' block it was possible to use cylinder bores of 90 mm or even 90.4 mm, which in conjunction with the un-altered stroke gave capacities of 1975 cc or 1995 cc respectively.

That, in itself, was remarkable enough, but the really sensational decision Hart made was to have these new blocks cast in aluminium alloy. Here, therefore, was not only an engine that could be enlarged right out to the class limit for sporting purposes, but one that was significantly (40 lb approximately) lighter as well.

Hart, being a modest, self-effacing fellow, never even mentioned this project to Ford, and when, early in 1972, Peter Ashcroft visited his workshops in connection with the forthcoming East African Safari, he tripped over—quite literally, he has assured me, more than once—a light-alloy block which Hart's mechanics had just finished machining. After his astonishment had subsided, and his adrenalin count had returned to normal, he quickly arranged to have it fitted to an

The internals of a late 1970s BDA engine, in 1.8-litre light-alloy cylinder block form

RS1600, equally as quickly showed it to Stuart Turner and Walter Hayes, and soon persuaded the powers-that-be to have it put into series production. The first production batch of blocks was sourced at Stirling Metals, and the light-alloy-block RS1600 road cars went on sale in the autumn of 1972. For those to whom such things matter, I should say that the chassis number at which light-alloy blocks took over from cast-iron blocks on RS1600 production was ATM.00112.

The light-alloy block which, because of its material, and because of the limited rate at which it was cast and machined, was more costly, was never applied to any other Escort except the RS1800 which replaced the RS1600 in 1975. In

Above A styling-studio picture of the first RS2000 project of 1972–73—here badged as a 'Puma'

Opposite Page A Mexico race at the Belgian Zolder circuit, with Simon Taylor of Autosport *leading this bunch*

81

A 1973 RS2000, as finished off in 'Special Build' at AVO, with flared arches and extra driving lamps, not forgetting the extra-wide wheels and tyres

summary, all 16-valve Escorts built after October 1972 were equipped with light-alloy cylinder blocks, but no other Escorts ever were.

As far as the RS1600 road-cars were concerned, this change made no difference to the rated power output of the engines, and the 40 lb weight reduction had almost no effect on the car's performance. Ford, however, were not about to pass on such a valuable improvement to the customer, especially as it was also accompanied by the fitting of sports road wheels, full carpeting, hazard-warning flashers and other details appropriate to the 1973 model-year programme; the price, therefore, went up from £1553 to £1704. (At the same time, incidentally, the cosmetic changes were also applied to the Mexico: the battery was re-located from its special position in the boot to the original 'standard' position under the bonnet, and the price rose from £1212 to £1229—a very minor impost indeed).

For the next 27 months, production of the RS1600 and Mexico models continued at the AVO building at South Ockendon with no more than minor changes, (unlike the mass-production versions of this very successful car these cars were never built in Germany), and it would be fair to say that demand for both fell away considerably in 1974. One reason was, of course, because of the great blow dealt to all performance cars by the psychological effects of the energy crisis and the rise in petrol prices—the other was undoubtedly due to internal competition from yet another new car, the Escort RS2000.

This model, as it turned out, was the most significant of all the special Escorts conceived in what I like to call the 'AVO years'. Stuart Turner had not only become the Director of Ford's motor sporting operations in Europe but, from June 1972 he had also taken over from Ray Horrocks as the manager of the entire AVO plant as well. It was after discussions with his staff, which still included Bob Howe (who had 'product planned' the very first Twin-Cam), with the Ford sales force, and particularly with the German branch of the company, that it became clear that there was an opportunity to produce yet another variety of RS Escort. What was needed, it seemed, was a car which was almost as fast as the RS1600, but one which was not nearly as complex, as expensive, or as difficult to keep in tune.

The answer, as any Escort-lover knows, was to develop the RS2000, which swopped revs and multi-valve cylinder heads for simplicity and a larger engine. The engine swop proposed discarding the 16-valve Cosworth-Ford BDA and sub-

Above *The RS2000 of 1973 in production form, complete with RS type cast-alloy road wheels*

Right *The RS2000 had a suitable boot-lid badge to give the game away. Like most early examples, this had left-hand drive*

stituting the entirely different single-overhead-cam Ford 'Pinto' unit instead. It sounds simple enough, but the complication was that the 'Pinto' engine was just that important bit larger—longer *and* taller—than the engine it displaced, and it needed considerable skill to shoe-horn it neatly into the Escort's unmodified engine bay. At the same time, AVO completely rethought their philosophy on suspension settings, and the result (helped along by one of Turner's protégés, Gerry Birrell, who was an expert car 'sorter' and young racing driver) was that the RS2000 was a much more refined and compliant machine than any of the previous cars had been.

The 'chassis' of the RS2000, the bodyshell, and the general layout were all very much as before, which is to say that the old Lotus-Cortina type of back axle was retained, with extra location by twin radius arms, and that vacuum servo-assisted front disc brakes were standardised, the engine and gearbox, however, were different. The engine

The rather high overhead-camshaft 'Pinto' 2-litre engine was something of a push-fit into the confines of the Escort bodyshell

Jackie Stewart and Graham Bridgewater (sales manager of AVO in 1973), posed with an early right-hand-drive example of the 1973 RS2000

itself was functionally the same as that fitted to current Cortina GTs and (from 1974) Capri GTs, which is to say that the single-overhead-camshaft design had been treated to a downdraught compound twin-choke Weber carburettor, a free-flow exhaust manifold (but still in cast-iron, rather than of tubular construction like the hottest Escorts), and a more sporting camshaft profile.

To clear the Escort's cross-member there was a different (cast-alloy) sump pan, this and a new light-alloy bell housing both helping to reduce weight and to raise a natural boom engine resonance from 5400 rpm to more than 6000 rpm. Because the power unit was rather large for the engine bay, the Cortina/Capri belt-driven fan had to be abandoned, and a Kenlowe electric fan was installed instead. The result was that peak power was marginally better: 100 bhp (DIN) at 5750 rpm, with peak torque of 108 lb ft at 3500 rpm.

The axle ratio was 3.54:1 compared with 3.77:1 on the other RS Escorts, but the gearbox was a standard Cortina unit in which the ratios were rather more widely spread than on the traditional 'Corsair 2000E' box of the other cars. There was no question of the boxes being closely related, incidentally, for even the casing was substantially different. AVO engineers had made minor changes to the gear selector linkage, and the result was a very smooth, short-action, 'flick switch' gear change movement.

To match this transplant and increase in refinement, the RS2000 was given the latest four stud cast-alloy 'RS' road wheels, a nice flat-rimmed special steering wheel and those sumptuous reclining RS seats—optional only on other RSs—as standard. The battery of the RS2000,

The interior and facia layout of the RS2000, considerably more plush than that of earlier Escort RS models, as proposed by Ford styling, but not adopted for production cars

incidentally, lived up front, and the spare wheel was now stowed in the standard recess supplied to the left of the Escort's boot floor, which brought it into line with Mexico installations. There was the usual choice of RS colour schemes and (unless you specifically asked for them to be deleted) there were distinctive RS2000 stripes on the bonnet and along the flanks; many customers, indeed, insisted on these rather garish details being deleted from their car's specification.

Here and there, to tailor the new model to its real objective as a fast road machine rather than a basic rally car, there was evidence of cost-cutting. The rear brakes, for instance, which had 9-in diameter drums and 1.75-in wide shoes on the RS1600/Mexico model, were 8 × 1.5 in on the RS2000.

Clearly, here was a car which could be built in considerable numbers and its appeal was likely to be even wider than that of the Mexico. The Germans, who had never taken to the earlier RS models, loved it, and immediately put in an order for 2000 cars. The result was that although the car was revealed at the beginning of July 1973, all the initial production was of left-hand-drive models for Germany, and the first UK deliveries were not made until October.

It had always been Ford's intention to homologate the RS2000 as a standard 'Group 1' touring car, for it had a 1993 cc engine, right up to the 2-litre class limit. However, even at the efficient little AVO plant, it took time for those 5000 cars to be assembled, and homologation was delayed until April 1974. Boreham, thereafter, had no real interest in the RS2000 for serious international competition work. However if the later German-developed twin-downdraught Solex carburettor system was installed it proved possible to extract 150 bhp in homologated 'Group

The RS2000 was available in a variety of colour schemes. In this black-and-white shot, the presence of the contrasting stripe is not at all obvious

1' form, from the tall 'Pinto' engine. In this guise, however, camshaft life was rather short—one long international event being about the limit before wear became too serious. Using this kit, which was approved just before the event started, Roger Clark and Gerry Marshall dominated proceedings in the 1974 Avon Tour of Britain, with Clark winning outright and Marshall following him home in second place.

The proof of the pudding, as they say, is in the performance, and the RS2000 certainly proved itself it be a remarkably well-developed and more simple substitute for the RS1600. *Autocar*'s test, published in October 1973, tells its own story, for their RS2000 had a maximum speed of 108 mph (just 5 mph less than that of the RS1600—and at a mere 5780 rpm), sprinted to 60 mph in 9.0 seconds,

A well-drilled circus act—Roger Clark (leading) and Gerry Marshall in the two works-entered RS2000s which dominated the BRSCCs Avon-Motor Tour of Britain in 1974

and to the quarter-mile marker in 17.1 seconds (both just fractionally slower than a standard RS1600), and recorded an overall fuel consumption figure of 26.6 mpg. All this, incidentally, in conjunction with considerably less noise and with a greater degree of mechanical refinement, for £1586 (which was a massive £278 *less* than the price of an RS1600).

The result, as far as AVO and Ford Rallye Sport dealers were concerned, was that demand for RS1600s slipped away, so that these cars were only sold to the potentially serious race and rally competitors who needed the ability (if they could find the money) to have their cars super-tuned to produce 230/240 bhp. The RS2000, however, was still more costly than the Mexico (£1586 compared with £1348) and did not begin to out-sell it until 1974, by which time the word had got around, and the first cars were making their reputations on the roads of Europe. As I have already explained in the Introduction, precise production figures are not available from Ford, but it does seem that once the RS2000 became freely available, it outsold the Mexico by about two to one.

In the meantime, however, the Yom Kippur war had erupted in the Middle East, and as a direct consequence the well-head posted price of crude oil had been increased by a factor of four. Not only did this mean that petrol and refined oil prices were soon to rise dramatically—in Britain petrol prices doubled within a year or so—but in the winter of 1973–74 there were potential shortages, and much talk about rationing. Throughout Europe, too, there was a rash of 'economy' speed limit legislation, not all of which has ever been rescinded. Most motor sport came to a halt during the winter, and things only truly began to get back to normal in the spring of 1974.

Although Ford were not deterred by this—it is now a matter of record that at the depths of this crisis they were actively considering ways of increasing the performance, the coverage, and the appeal of their cars—it is a fact that their overall sales were affected. The little RS Escort production plant, AVO at South Ockendon, bucked that trend and sold many more cars in 1974 than it had in 1973, mainly due to the popularity of the new RS2000.

With a re-styled range of Escorts due to be

revealed in January 1975, Ford clearly had a problem and they made what many, to this day, see as a misguided decision. With their 'bread-and-butter' Escort factories operating well under capacity and likely to remain so for a time, they decided to cut out various frivolities—and one of them was the AVO plant. When the original-shape Escort was withdrawn from production towards the end of 1974, it was decided, the AVO plant would also be closed down. There would, indeed, be new-shape RS Escorts, but they were planned for assembly on the normal mass-production Escort assembly lines.

In motor and sporting enthusiasts' circles the news, when it broke in December 1974, caused something of an uproar. Ever since the AVO factory opened in 1970, after all, Ford had made much of its 'cottage industry' flexible appeal. Here, now, was a complete change of attitude, with the public being told that such a plant was 'no longer viable'. When the last of the old-style bodies had been used up at the end of January 1975, the 100 hourly-paid workers would be re-deployed (mainly at Dagenham) and the staff operation would gradually be run down after work on the new models had been completed.

One result, as far as Ford dealers were concerned, was that there was an instant upsurge of interest in Mexicos and RS2000s. As the new Escorts were revealed, it was made clear that there would be no new RS models before 1976 and this led to many customers scrambling to buy up the remaining dealer stocks of old-shape Mark I Mexicos and RS2000s. Secondhand prices soared, and it was in 1975 that the RS2000 took on the mantle of an 'instant classic'.

It is worth noting, in passing, that although officially speaking there was no such thing as an RS Escort which was other than a two-door

saloon, the little factory built a couple of Mexico estates for evaluation purposes (*Sunday Times* motoring correspondent Judith Jackson used one for a time), and at least eight four-door Mexicos were built to satisfy a Liverpool police order.

In spite of the internal and external protests, there was no last-minute reprieve for the AVO production facility. When I visited South Ockendon in 1977, more than two years after RS Escort production had ceased, the merry-go-round track was still there, inanimate, but I was assured that it was 'in mothballs'. The space had returned to an earlier use—for spare parts storage—but I was also assured that it was possible, if necessary, to bring the assembly line back to life. Alas, this has never been done.

'Ello, 'ello, 'ello, what's this 'ere. Actually, it's one of the very few Mexico police cars supplied for fast patrol use in 1973

Chapter 5
RS1800-Old wine, New bottle

Although not many people realised it, the introduction of new Escorts for the last half of the 1970s was a two-stage operation. No one could miss the new body style made public in January 1975, but few ever found out that significant floor pan and rear suspension changes had been phased in to the old-shape Escorts during 1973, the main object being to improve the operation and durability of the rear dampers. A look underneath at—say—a late model RS2000 Mark I and an early RS1600 will pinpoint the differences.

Even the introduction of the new-look Escorts was not a straightforward, once-and-for-all affair. The mass-market examples were revealed in January, with only a promise that new RS models would be announced 'later'. The new sporting Escorts—actually titled RS1800 and RS2000—were first shown at Geneva in March 1975, but the RS1800 did not, in reality, go on sale until June 1975, and the sale of RS2000s was actually delayed until January 1976. This, of course, explains the boom in obsolete RS2000s mentioned in the previous chapter.

The RS1800—first sold in June 1975, and officially withdrawn in September 1977—was the rarest of all the RS Escorts built between 1968 and 1980. In almost every way, except for the fact that it simply had to be on sale to allow the new-shape cars to be raced or rallied by the factory and by private owners alike, the RS1800 was something of an indulgence, for previous experience with the Mark I cars had shown that the vast majority of customers would plump for an RS2000 if they wanted equivalent performance, or go for a Mexico if they wanted low cost and simple engineering.

Nevertheless, I ought to scotch the rumour that the RS1800, as a road car did not really exist, for this was demonstrably untrue. It *was* true that it was extremely difficult to get hold of one in that first year, 1975, and it was always true that it had to be ordered, as such machines were never held in stock either by Ford or by RS dealers; there is no doubt however, that a substantial number were

Mark II, new style Escorts, taking shape at Saarlouis in 1976. It was in this factory that RS1800s and RS2000 Mk IIs were built

95

built. Just how many is impossible to state, mainly because lots of RS1800s were quite literally 'created' by experts outside the factory using brand new bodyshells and all the appropriate components. At one time, and for competition purposes only, Ford went so far as to advertise the availability of trimmed bodyshells so that new competition cars could be built up very speedily by their RS dealers and private owners.

Even so, Ford agree that as far as they were concerned, the RS1800 was something of an oddity—of which the very first few were assembled partly at Halewood and partly in the small sections of AVO which remained open at South Ockendon; the rest in production (in 1976 and 1977) took the form of incomplete Mexicos being engined and rebadged at AVO before delivery to the customers.

The specification of the road-car very carefully took note of what the sporting regulations might require in 1978 and beyond, for proposals for change already existed in 1974. The RS1800, indeed, came into existence as an 'homologated' competition car by the process known as 'evolution' from the old RS1600 and always used that car's homologation form and number. Quite openly and officially, a 1835 cc engine was approved in January 1975 and a new-shape body style was approved in May 1975—both before the unmodified road car actually went on sale to the public.

The important mechanical basis of the car was very similar indeed to that of the RS1600, except that the engine was enlarged and a different gearbox was specified. Both these changes were standardised on the road-cars because of particular fears about impending competition regulations. The rules regarding evolution, in sporting terms, were that an engine could only be enlarged by a maximum of 15 per cent. If that figure was applied to the RS1600's 1601 cc, the result was 1841 cc, so by choosing a new cylinder bore of 86.75 mm, and by reverting to the 'standard' 'Kent' stroke dimension of 77.62 mm, Ford were able to produce a 1835 cc 16-valve BDA engine, which was very close indeed to the sporting limit, and which was, incidentally, misquoted by *Autocar* in their official road test of July 1975 as 1845 cc, not once but several times!

At the same time it was decided to cut the cost of the engine, make servicing easier for RS dealers *and* owners, and improve the low-speed pulling of the unit, by discarding the twin side-draught dual-choke Weber carburettors in favour of a new inlet manifold and a single downdraught compound dual-choke 32/36 DGAV Weber instrument. The result was that the RS1800's maximum

power output was 115 bhp (DIN) at 6000 rpm (5 bhp *less* than that of the RS1600), but peak torque was 120 lb ft at 4000 rpm, an 8 lb ft increase over the obsolete model. Road tests showed just how effective the juggling of engine capacity and carburation had been for pulling power in top gear was virtually constant all the way from 20 mph to 80 mph, at which point adverse aerodynamics began to get in the way.

Another rule change suggested for 1978 was that substitute gearboxes (for competition use) might be banned. This meant that the bomb-proof ZF box might be outlawed—and as an 'in-case' change, Ford therefore specified their larger 'medium uprated' four-speed all-synchromesh gearbox on the RS1800—a design never used on any other Escort of any type. In mass-production form, this was normally found on 2.5-litre Granadas and 2.3-litre 'Pinto' engined cars, and was blessed with close top, third and second gear ratios, but quite a low first gear, In fact, the threatened legislation never affected Ford, and the use of this gearbox was therefore not essential; as far as RS1800 road-car users are con-

A series of shots showing development testing of an early Mk II Escort RS model at Bagshot. Bill Meade is driving, and that looks like John Taylor in the passenger seat

cerned, it meant that they had a strong transmission with a perfectly acceptable change.

Visually, and in comparison with other Escorts of the same type, the RS1800 was recognisable only by the deep front 'chin' spoiler (which it shared with the RS Mexico of 1976–78), the boot lid rubberised spoiler which is shared with the RS Mexico and the 1976–80 RS2000, by the twin-blue stripes along the flanks, and by the use of RS1800 transfers (metal badges were out of fashion by this time) on the rear wings. If you looked even more carefully you could see the '1.8' badges on the front wings. Out of sight was the reversion to a mass-production layout of the engine bay, with the battery up front alongside the engine, and with the sculptured steel 'sports' spare wheel tucked into the boot floor recess at the near side.

Inside the car, the plushiest type of trim and fittings were found on the RS1800 Custom (which, at £2957 included the superb RS reclining seats, a centre console, extra instruments and a facia-mounted clock. There was also the option of the basic RS1800, which cost £2825 and lacked these 'comfort' options.

As with the Twin-Cam, so with the RS1600 and the RS1800, Roger Clark was the first to record a rally victory. HHJ 700N was his famous 1975 RS1800, here seen winning the Granite City Rally on its very first outing

As one would expect from a car which was virtually as powerful, and almost the same weight, as the superseded RS1600, the performance of the standard RS1800 road-car was about the same as that of the earlier car. Maximum speed was 111 mph (at 6000 rpm—the rev-limiter not cutting in until 6500 rpm on the test car)—0–60 mph took nine seconds, the standing start quarter mile just less than 17 seconds, and typical fuel consumption of Premium 4-star petrol was about 28 mpg. The RS1800, in fact, was a surprisingly fuel-efficient car of its type, which speaks volumes for the 16-valve Cosworth design. The engine changes from RS1600 to RS1800, incidentally, had involved a drop in compression ratio from 10:1 to 9:1, and there was no longer any question of cars being able to use other than 4-star fuel.

The first batch of RS1800s was manufactured from cars which started their lives as Escort 1600 Sports at Halewood—for the new-shape bodies were much less special than the old ones had been, without flared wheel arches, and with little extra stiffening—while very limited production was transferred to the German (Saarlouis) plant from the beginning of 1976, at the same time as the RS Mexico and RS2000 Mark 2 models began to be built. It was no longer necessary for engine production to be farmed out on a major contract, since quantities were much lower than before, so when a number of 'road-car' RS1800 units were needed they were speedily built up by the Brian Hart organisation.

Even though the Escort was not due to be discontinued in favour of an all-new front-wheel-drive model until 1980, and the 16-valve engined car was likely to be Ford's major competition car until that time, the RS1800 road car was dropped in the autumn of 1977. This was done, not because

From its second outing, HHJ 700N was placarded with Cossack sponsorship, and Roger Clark is here seen on his way to winning the Welsh International Rally of 1975

the car could not be sold any more, but because there was really no market need for it any more. For road-car use it was matched by the latest shovel-nosed RS2000 (described in the next chapter), and for competition use it had already been replaced by another 'model'—the Escort RS.

Even though the 'Escort RS' (I use inverted commas because in production car terms it was very difficult indeed to define it at all) was not sold for normal road use, I ought to describe it with some care to show how things at Ford had evolved and the rules of competition changed—in other words, how the target shifted.

Earlier in the chapter I mentioned that new rules were being considered for 1978. Although this was perfectly true, the *actual* rules which came into force in that year did not have the same limits, or the same effect on Ford. Fortunately, by 1977, so many RS1800s had been prepared up to the limit of the existing (old-type) regulations that enough of them were in existence for a new homologation application to be made.

The RS Mexico or 'Mk II' Mexico as it is more familiarly known, was only available from 1976 to 1978

The Escort RS, which was homologated in April 1977, on the basis that 400 near-identical models had already been completed since the beginning of 1975, came into existence by an inspired and perfectly logical administrative process master-minded by Peter Ashcroft, and carried out for him by his paper work expert John Griffiths. The 'new car' (for I 'quote' this advisedly, as no new model was involved) merely brought together everything in the fully-prepared Escort RS1800 competition car which had previously been optional, pointed out that the necessary number of such cars had already been built, and homologated the beast as a 400-off Group 4 car.

Thus it was that the Escort RS took over, in competition terms, from the RS1800, which made the RS1800 redundant. The Escort RS (homologation form No 650) had a 90 mm bore, 1975 cc light-alloy engine with twin side-draught dual-choke Weber carburettors, a five-speed ZF gearbox, and a heavy-duty 'Atlas' type of back axle complete with limited slip differential. Front and rear wheel ventilated disc brakes were standardised, as were front shock absorbers of adjustable length and a rear suspension which included twin pairs of trailing arms and a Panhard rod for axle location. Magnesium alloy Minilite road wheels were also specified in a number of rim widths and to cover them there were metal wheel arch extensions. In addition, the engine was treated to a dry sump kit (whose large oil tank lived in the boot, along with the battery, a foam-filled fuel tank [choice of capacities], the two spare wheels and an oil cooler), while a full roll-cage, with 14 fixing points to the bodyshell, was also specified. As much trim and furnishing as possible was discarded, and as far as the Escort RS was concerned there was no rear seat.

Such cars were, and still are (as these words are written in the spring of 1981) race and rally winners and even though the rear-wheel-drive Escort was phased out of production in 1980, some specialists are still creating Escort RS models from their component parts. I would not be at all surprised if such cars are competitive until the mid-1980s.

Although this is not strictly a book about competition cars, I feel that I should mention that the 'works' Escort RS models which won the Constructors' World Rally Championship for Ford in 1979, (the year in which team members Bjorn Waldegard and Hannu Mikkola were also first and second in the Drivers' Championship), were

John Griffiths, of the Boreham Competitions Department, who looked after the homologation process which helped to make the team's rally cars into world Championship winners

103

eventually given *long-distance* 1995 cc BDA engines producing more than 270 bhp at 9000 rpm, which is a staggering 135 bhp/litre. In that state, they can still be started from cold after a night in the open in wintry conditions, and can still be pottered through heavy traffic with few signs of temperament and none of overheating. The BDA engine is a magnificent unit (and its life is by no means over yet . . .), and the Escort RS was, and is, a quite remarkable car.

All this, however, should not obscure the fact that the more commercially important Mark II RS Escorts were the Mexico and the RS2000 and it is to these models that I must now turn my attention. If the RS1800 was something of an anonymous-looking road burner, the RS2000 was anything but that. With its flamboyant wedge-nose looks, it was a very obvious, and a very worthy, world-beater.

Above *Hannu Mikkola and Arne Hertz, winning the 1979 Lombard-RAC Rally, making it eight successive Escort victories in that event, clinching the World Championship of Makes for that year, and providing a worthy swansong for the all-conquering 'works' Escorts*

Left *A rally prepared example of the BDA engine in full dry-sump, 2-litre form. This particular engine was prepared by Swindon Engines*

105

Chapter 6
RS2000-the wedge-nosed success

The decision to close down production of RS Escorts at the AVO plant at South Ockendon when the old models ran out at the end of 1974, was clearly a hasty last-minute move and threw the forward development of new RS models into disarray. Not only would it now be necessary to find a new home for new-shape RS models—if there *were* to be any new-shape models—but these cars would now have to be designed so that they could be assembled with very little disturbance to mass-production lines.

In view of all this, therefore, it was no surprise to those of us who are dedicated Ford-watchers, to be invited to the press launch of the new-style Escorts and find very little evidence of new RS models. Just one hastily-assembled (non-running) RS1800 was on display, decked out as an RAC Rally entry for Timo Makinen, and that was all. Furthermore, at the time it was stated that new RS1800 and RS2000 models would follow 'later', that they would be assembled at Halewood, and it was also tacitly made clear that there would be no more Mexicos.

The 'later' turned out to be the Geneva Motor Show in March 1975 when both cars appeared. It soon became clear, however, that the launch was premature. As I have already written, the first few

The distinctive shape of the droop-snoot RS2000 Mk II of 1976–80, the most versatile and numerous of all Escort RS models

RS1800s were not ready until June 1975, while the RS2000 was not available for sale until January 1976.

It was, however, well worth waiting for. The new RS2000 turned out to be the only RS Escort which Ford stylists were ever allowed to re-shape—albeit not totally—and with hindsight it seems that this was a deliberate attempt to educate the Ford-buying public to the idea of buying wedge-nosed cars. Apart from some worthwhile mechanical improvements, the new RS2000 was instantly (and pleasantly) recognisable by its unique wedge-style nose, which

Above *The slickly styled instrument panel and control layout of the 1976 Mk II RS Mexico with—in this case—special bucket seats. The RS2000 layout was rather more complete than this.*

Right *The RS2000 when fitted with the optional X-Pack features of a bigger front spoiler and the Zakspeed-style wheel arch extensions*

featured four headlamps recessed in an extended, flexible polyurethane nose-cone which also incorporated the front bumper. It was unfortunate for Ford that there was a very similar (in style, and in marketing intent) Vauxhall Firenza on sale at the time, and the 'droop-snoot' nickname of that car was soon applied to the RS2000 as well.

The wedge nose, which incorporated a sizeable chin spoiler, along with a rubberised spoiler across the rear of the boot lid, was certainly not there just for show, as Ford's claims (and practical experience by testers) made clear. The RS2000 had a 16 per cent better drag coefficient, 25 per cent less front end lift, and 60 per cent lower rear end lift than the conventional Escorts—and this was an obvious pointer to the way future Fords were likely to improve on fuel-efficiency. If only we had known; the Fiesta, then the Granada and finally the new front-drive Escort, would all have similar, but less dramatic, wedge noses to emphasise the family likeness.

Mechanically the RS2000 was similar to the obsolete old-shape model, but thanks to the use of a special high-efficiency exhaust system (which says very little for the standard item!) the 1993 cc engine now produced 110 bhp (DIN) at 5500 rpm, while torque had been boosted to 119 lb ft at 4000 rpm. The light-alloy bell housing and the four-speed all-synchromesh gearbox, along with the 3.54:1 axle ratio, were all as before, but on this model there was a wide flat plastic air cleaner for the carburettor on top of the engine's cam cover.

The most obvious individuality was in the front styling, and a careful look revealed that the standard steel outer wings of the normal Escorts had been cut back and allied to a longer and differently profiled steel bonnet, so that the one-piece plastic nose-cone could be smoothly incorporated. All the inner panels, however, were unchanged. When the car was revealed in March 1975 it was stated to have 5.5 in rim width sculptured steel wheels like those of the Mark I cars, with alloy rims as optional extras, but by the time it was actually put on sale the 6.0 in rim cast-alloy wheels had been standardised.

After the new car had first been shown at Geneva there was a wait—a long wait. Then, in October, the production-standard RS2000s were exhibited at the Paris and Earls Court motor shows and we all thought that deliveries were about to begin. In the event, these were delayed until January 1976, when there was a real surprise—not only was the new-shape RS2000 every bit as fast and nice as we had all hoped it would be, but it was also accompanied by a new stablemate—the RS Mexico!

The new RS Mexico (or, as it was most often called by enthusiasts, the Mark II Mexico) showed all the signs of being a hurriedly developed model. No advance publicity was generated for what was the least expensive of the new generation of RS Escorts, and hindsight suggests that its specification (and its selling price) were never truly placed at the right point to generate a lot of sales.

What was an RS Mexico? Firstly, it was a model only available between January 1976 and the autumn of 1978—less than three years. Secondly, it always lived in the shadow of the RS2000, which seemed to offer more performance *and* better value for money. Thirdly, an RS Mexico was an amalgam of RS1800 looks and quasi-RS2000 mechanicals.

To be specific, the bodyshell, the trim, furnishings, front and rear suspension and brakes of the RS Mexico were all those of the RS1800—or, rather, as I have already explained, the RS1800s retained all these parts when they were 'created'

by being re-engined as production progressed. Visually, the RS Mexico had the standard squared-up Mark II nose styling, and the rubberised tail spoiler of the RS1800, while it had the side stripes of the Escort 1300 and 1600 Sport models, but with a 'Mexico' badge on each rear wing hard by the tail lamps. The cast-alloy road wheels of the RS2000 were standardised, but the front seats were low-backed competition-style items and different from those of the RS2000.

The gearbox was that of the RS2000, as was the back axle ratio of 3.54:1 and the only major difference was the engine. This was of the same 'Pinto' family as that fitted to the RS2000, which is to say that it had a single overhead camshaft and

The instrument panel of the RS2000 which should be compared with that of the RS Mexico on page 108. This is a left-hand-drive car with a Km/h speedometer

111

valve operation by interposed fingers, but its bore and stroke were 87.65 × 66 mm, and its swept volume was 1593 cc. This was an engine size found in Cortinas and Capris, but the power output in RS Mexico tune was 95 bhp (DIN) at 5750 rpm, and maximum torque was 92 lb ft developed at 4000 rpm. A back-to-back comparison with the Capri S (88 bhp at 5700 rpm, 93 lb ft torque at 4000 rpm) emphasised that although the same valve gear and cam profiles had been used, the RS Mexico had a more efficient exhaust system than that of the Capri S, and one which also seemed to turn it into a much more 'peaky' unit. Naturally the RS Mexico was homologated for sporting purposes—as an evolution of the Escort 1600 Sport, under FIA No. 5586, in Group 1.

Calculations suggest that the RS Mexico was a 100 mph-plus performer—it had more power than the old-type Mexico, and had better drag characteristics—but we will never know the precise and actual figures for Ford never provided

Tiny detailing was so carefully done on RS Escorts. This RS2000 Mk II has Zakspeed-style extended wheel arches

The original Ford publicity shot of the Mk II RS2000 issued in 1975

a car for test by the major motoring magazines. Right from the start, it seems, it became clear that the RS Mexico was by no means as flexible and easy to drive as the old Mexico had been, nor as satisfying as the RS2000.

There was also the double problem of the presence in the 'bread-and-butter' Escort range of the 1600 Sport (which was really a less-specialised successor to the old Mexico with the same sort of performance). It had an initial price £510 (£1933 compared with £2443) lower than that of the RS Mexico. Unfortunately, the RS Mexico seemed to be something of an 'orphan' model right from the start. It was a car which seemed to arrive on the scene rather apologetically, which never seemed to be backed up by any aggressive selling and one in which neither Ford nor any circuit owner or rally series organiser showed much interest. Once the original Mexico had appeared, there always seemed to be a place for it in the sporting scene; for the RS (or Mark II) Mexico, there was none.

Once the complete range of Mark II RS Escorts had been put on sale in January 1976, Escort enthusiasts were offered this choice of cars:

RS Mexico, 1593 cc single cam, 95 bhp, £2443 total
RS2000, 1993 cc single cam, 110 bhp, £2857 total
RS1800, 1835 cc twin-cam, 16-valve, 115 bhp, £2925 total
RS1800 Custom 1835 cc twin-cam, 16-valve, 115 bhp, £3049 total

None of these prices stayed put for long, however, for Britain was in the middle of a frightening period of high inflation, and all the motor manufacturers took the opportunity of pushing their prices up, a few per cent at a time, at three month intervals.

It is interesting, incidentally, to pause for a moment and see what the major rivals were

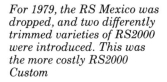

For 1979, the RS Mexico was dropped, and two differently trimmed varieties of RS2000 were introduced. This was the more costly RS2000 Custom

offering in this sporting category at the time. Vauxhall's 'droop-snoot' Firenza had not been a success and had already been withdrawn, and the fuel-injected VW Golf GTI was not yet available in Britain. The obvious competition came from Opel with the 1.9-litre Kadett GT/E at £2685 (but it was only available in left-hand-drive form, at first), from Triumph with the four-door 16-valve Dolomite Sprint (2-litre) at £3083, and—if you were well-off and didn't want to go rallying—the 2-litre BMW 320 at £3349.

Compared with RS Escorts, all of which could be, and often were, modified with competitions in mind, the only face-to-face rival was the Opel Kadett GT/E. In fairness, I have to admit that in Group 1 competition the GT/E was even more successful in the next few years than was the RS2000—however the only car which could match the overall worth of the RS1800 (or its descendant, the Escort RS) was the Fiat 131 Abarth Rallye saloon, which was a similar type of 'homologation special' but one which was never actively put on sale in Britain. From 1976 to 1980, Ford's biggest battles were always with the 131 Abarths, and it was either Ford or Fiat who dominated the World Championship rallying scene during those years.

A survey of the technical press road tests of the RS2000 confirms that AVO's product planners, designers, and development engineers had got the concept absolutely right, for it was a great success with all of them. If we can assume that the cars loaned to the press were in normal, standard, healthy tune, the figures they produced certainly proved that the claims for the revised aerodynamics were accurate, and that the 1993 cc single cam engine was at least as lusty as advertised. It is very interesting indeed to compare selected figures obtained by *Autocar* with their RS2000 in January 1976, and their RS1800 of July 1975:

	RS2000	RS1800
Engine power (DIN bhp)	110 at	115 at
	5500 rpm	6000 rpm
Unladen weight (lb)	2075	2016
Maximum speed (mph)	109	111
0–60 mph acceleration (sec)	8.6	9.0
0–100 mph acceleration (sec)	33.6	32.9
Standing $\frac{1}{4}$-mile (sec)	16.7	16.9
Overall fuel consumption (mpg)	24.7	26.5
'Typical' consumption (mpg)	27.0	28.0
Mpg at steady 70 mph	27.6	30.8

—all this from the RS2000 with great flexibility, potentially great reliability from near-standard components, and at a very reasonable price! It begged the question that there was no commercial market for the RS1800—a hunch backed up by the fact that very few people preferred one when faced with the attractions of the RS2000.

Once launched, at the beginning of 1976, the RS2000 became available in considerable numbers. Along with the Mexico and the rare RS1800, the RS2000 was built on the production lines at the West German Escort factory at Saarlouis, only being side-tracked towards the end of the process for the special engine, transmission and suspension items to be fitted, not forgetting the fitting of the distinctive flexible plastic nose cone.

For sporting purposes, Group 1 homologation of the RS2000 was achieved immediately after its launch, for it was truly an 'evolution' of the original RS2000. It was not a car for which Ford's 'works' team at Boreham had many plans, though many useful special items were made available including the heavy-duty 'Atlas' axle from the RS1800 and the twin Solex engine tune of the original RS2000.

Just to prove their point, Ford produced three 'works' RS2000s for the 1976 Texaco Tour of Britain, which resulted in an outright win for the

You specify as much or as little as you like

With Series X kits you can add authentic Rallye Sport style and performance to your RS2000. You can specify more power, bigger brakes, stiffer suspension, lightweight alloy wheels, airdam, spoiler, wheel arches — with Series X you make as much or as little change as you like

Nothing could be more flexible. Be an individual, go Series X!

The RS2000 custom illustrated is fitted with the following combination of Series X parts:

'Zakspeed' wing extensions with front spoiler together with 7½ x 13" RS alloy wheels and 225/60 tyres
Hood locking kit
Group one, twin carburettor engine with special air cleaner
Rocket gear box
Limited slip differential
Gas-filled suspension with increased capacity springs
Ventilated disc brakes with heavy duty pads and shoes

In 1980, Ford promoted their X-Pack concept very hard, and this advertisement shows the scope and nature of parts which were available for the RS2000

young Ari Vatanen in a car sponsored by the Allied Polymer Group. Murphy's Law, however, also intervened, for two of the three cars blew their clutches, comprehensively, during the very first test and caused their drivers—Roger Clark and Timo Makinen—to retire at once.

Sales of the RS2000 went from strength to

strength in 1976–78—many more were sold in West Germany and in other European countries, incidentally, than Ford had ever achieved with the original RS2000s or Mexicos—and more than 12,000 were sold in that phenomenal first year, but the Mexico never truly made an impact. Ford, therefore, decided to make a major realignment in their offerings. By the end of 1977 the RS1800 had already been dropped (the 'Custom' trim option, indeed, had been discontinued at the end of 1976), and in 1978 the axe fell over the RS Mexico.

In September 1978, the realignment was made public. The RS Mexico, whose final price had been £3632 compared with the £4330 then asked for the RS2000, was dropped, and no one seemed to miss it. (The Escort 1600 Sport, incidentally, cost £3142.) Henceforth, the RS2000 was marketed in two versions, mechanically identical, but with considerable differences in trim and visual equipment—as the RS2000 and the RS2000 Custom, priced at £3902 and £4416 respectively. The new 'base-model' RS2000, therefore, was craftily priced £270 above the RS Mexico for which it was the effective replacement, but was £428 cheaper than the 1978-model RS2000 and £514 cheaper than the new RS2000 Custom.

Trim and fittings of the 1979-model 'base' RS2000 were much as before, except that 1600 Sport-style low-back reclining seats and 5.5-in sculptured steel road wheels were specified. The RS2000 Custom, on the other hand, which cost a mere £86 more than the last of the 1978 models, had prestigious high-back Recaro reclining seats, 6.0-in rim cast-alloy road wheels as before, a remote-control driver's door mirror, and bronze-tinted glass all round.

It was about this time, too, that rally watchers saw their first 'flat-nosed' RS2000s in action.

These, quite literally, were RS2000s with RS1800/Mexico-style standard-shape noses—in other words, without the refinement of the bendy-plastic four-headlamp wedge nose—which were a little bit lighter *and* cheaper to repair after an accident than the original variety. RS2000s in this shape were never offered by Ford in Europe, but RS2000s assembled in Australia and South Africa *were* built like that, and an homologation amendment had to be put through to cater for such cars. Once this change was made public, several British and European RS2000 rally cars reverted to the old-style flat nose; when decked out in a sponsor's livery the only way to recognise such an RS2000 from a Group 4 Escort RS was by its wheels (Group 1 cars have to use the standard issue), by its lack of wheel arch extensions, and by the less strident engine note. Cars which won the Group 1 category in the Lombard-RAC Rallies of 1979 and 1980 both featured flat noses.

It was only after driving the latest RS2000 that one realised how Ford's approach to such machines had changed so much in less than ten years. The earliest Twin-Cams had been searingly fast by the standards of the late 1960s, had been rather sparsely equipped and had been filled with suspension developed at Boreham, whose engineers liked their cars to have final oversteer, and to have a very speedy response to steering movements.

The first of the RS2000s, announced in 1973, had been much more civilised than this, though its links with the Twin-Cam, the RS1600 and the Mexico were all obvious. The new range of RS Escorts and most especially the RS2000s, was even more civilised in road-car tune. The miracle was that Ford got their hunches absolutely right. The world of motoring, it seemed, was good and ready to buy truly fast little cars with a great deal

RS becomes XR. The effective successor to the rear-drive Escort RS models was the front-wheel-drive Escort XR3. Even though it only has a 1.6-litre engine, it has nearly as much performance as the old 2-litre RS2000. Such is progress

of refinement and civilised equipment—sales of RS2000s proved this.

It was probably inevitable, therefore, that the down-market 1979 RS2000 would not take many sales, and that the RS2000 Custom would be most popular. The breakdown of sales varied from region to region, and even from dealer to dealer, but it seems that up to 80 per cent of all 1979 and 1980 RS2000 sales were of the 'Custom' variety. The more percipient Ford RS dealers bought up as many RS2000 Customs as they could when production began to tail off in 1980, but they also made sure that their stocks of 'base' models were kept down.

To most people's amazement, this last generation of 'hot' Escorts was even taken up by a particular type of business user—one who would have loved a sports car if only his company, or his partners, had allowed it, and one who wanted all the performance but little of the bulk of something like a Granada. Such a buyer loved the plush form-hugging seats, the direct steering, and the responsive handling of an RS2000, even if he did not, perhaps, like the heavy low-speed steering, or the stubby little gear lever and short changing movements. Certainly he appreciated the fact that the car could be cruised at anything up to 90 mph or more if the law was not looking, at which speed it was only just possible to listen to the radio which was standard equipment. It was precisely this type of owner, too, who didn't mind the fact that rear seat space was limited by a lack of leg room, and by the high-backed Recaro seats—in almost every case, he treated his RS2000 as a 2+2 sports car with a closed roof.

For a short time the appearance of the special four-headlamp nose caused controversy but there were no other disadvantages. The four-headlamp installation, complete with halogen bulbs, was significantly better than any Escort two-headlamp system: the aerodynamic performance was quite definitely better than before, there was virtually no weight penalty and the extra front overhang was a mere 6.5 inches.

Nevertheless, by the time the two-model RS2000 was announced in the autumn of 1978, it was already known that the model range was becoming obsolete. Ford had launched their first front-wheel-drive car, the Fiesta, with great success (and great panache) in 1976, and by 1978 they made no secret of the fact that their next Escort would also have front-wheel drive. Worse, they had also carried out a progressive running down of the entire Rallye Sport operation, and long before the rear-drive Escorts were discontinued they had let it be known that there would be no more special 'RS' models for the time being.

In the event, the last RS2000s were built in the summer of 1980, although the last of all were not actually delivered until 1981. I have even heard of someone buying an RS2000 and resolving not to register it until 1 August 1981, thus making him the proud owner of an 'X-Registered' RS2000. At the time of writing, no direct replacement for this fine car has yet appeared, though in all practical and performance respects except for handling and exclusivity, the front-wheel drive Escort XR3 is an attractive substitute.

The effective life of the specialised RS Escorts, therefore, was a mere 12 years and there has been such a change in market demand and economic realities in that period that there may never be any true successors to the breed. Fortunately, many have survived in good condition (if you find a genuine RS1800 road car which has never been used in competition, you have a real collector's piece), and enthusiasts' clubs have already sprung up to cater for them. As far as Ford were concerned, the cars may never have made much money, but their effect on the company's image was profound. Every Ford built in the 1980s is a better car for the enthusiast than its 1960s equivalent, and we should all be grateful for that. The RS Escorts take much of the credit.

The engine bay of the transverse-engined front-wheel drive Escort XR3 of 1981. Will more and yet more sporting versions of this car (and its new 'Bridgend' engine) be developed?

Specifications

FORD ESCORT TWIN-CAM
Period produced: January 1968 to April 1971

Engine

Type	Four cylinders, in line, with twin overhead camshaft cylinder head and opposed valves. Ford, modified by Lotus
Bore, stroke & capacity	82.55 × 72.8 mm = 1558 cc (3.25 × 2.87 in = 95.2 cu in)
Compression ratio	9.5:1
Cylinder head	Aluminium alloy, with cross-flow breathing and individual inlet and exhaust ports. Part-spherical combustion chamber, with inlet and exhaust valves symmetrically disposed at included angle of 54 degrees. Two camshafts mounted in cylinder head, driven by roller chain
Cylinder block	Modified Ford item, combined with crankcase, in thin-wall cast-iron, with no cylinder liners
Crankshaft	In cast-iron, fully counterweighted, statically and dynamically balanced, and carried in five main bearings. No crankshaft damper on standard engine. Vandervell lead-indium bearings
Pistons	Light alloy, with three rings—two compression and one oil scraper.
Carburation	Twin horizontal double-choke Weber 40DCOE carburettors on inlet manifold cast integrally with cylinder head
Power output	106 bhp (net) at 6000 rpm.; maximum torque 107 lb ft at 4500 106 bhp (net) at 6000 rpm.; maximum torque 107 lb ft at 4500 rpm. Electronic rev-limiter in the distributor set at 6500 rpm

Transmission

Type	Four-speed, all synchromesh, manual gearbox, of Ford design, with remote-control selection and centre gear change
Internal ratios	1.00, 1.40, 2.01, 2.97, reverse 3.32:1
Rear axle	Hypoid bevel, 3.78:1
Propeller shaft	Single piece, no centre bearing

(Note: Alternative gearbox and rear axle ratios were available for competition purposes)

Chassis and suspension

Type	Pressed-steel unit-construction bodyshell in two-door saloon car style, modified from normal mass-production Ford Escort design. All structural stress-carrying members built into bodyshell
Front suspension	Independent, by coil springs on MacPherson struts, track control arms, and anti-roll bar doubling as section of bottom 'wishbone'. Telescopic hydraulic dampers built into struts
Steering	Rack and pinion, available in left-hand or right-hand drive layouts
Rear suspension	Live axle, half-elliptic leaf springs, twin trailing arms for location, and telescopic hydraulic dampers
Wheels & tyres	Pressed-steel wheels, with four fixing studs: 13 in diameter and 5.5-in rim width. 165-13-in radial ply tyres
Brakes	Disc brakes at the front wheels, drum brakes at the rear: hydraulically operated and with vacuum servo assistance: 9.62-in diameter front discs 9 × 1.75-in rear drums with leading and trailing shoes. Front swept area 190 sq in, rear swept area 96 sq in, total 286 sq in

Bodywork

Single body style, pressed-steel two-door saloon, differing from standard Escort by having reinforced 'heavy duty' features, and flared wheel arches to clear larger tyres. All-steel panels and glass windows—some competition cars with light alloy or glass-fibre panels, and Perspex windows

Major dimensions

Wheelbase	7ft 10.5 in (2400 mm)
Track, front	4 ft 3.7 in (1310 mm)
Track, rear	4 ft 4 in (1320 mm)
Overall length	13 ft 0.6 in (3980 mm)
Overall width	5 ft 1.8 in (1570 mm)
Overall height	4 ft 5 in (1350 mm)
Turning circle	29 ft 0 in (8.8 m)
Kerb weight (approx)	1730 lb (785 kg)

Development changes

Through the life of the car, mechanical changes were minor, and body amendments were made at the same time as mass-production Escorts were modified. In September 1968 there were minor trim changes, and from July 1969 circular quartz-halogen headlamps replaced original rectangular types. More minor trim changes followed in autumn 1970

Basic prices in Great Britain
From

January 1968	£879	October 1969	£951	April 1971	£1106
May 1968	£910	April 1970	£989		
October 1968	£915	October 1970	£1042		

FORD ESCORT RS1600
Period produced: January 1970 to December 1974
(From November 1970, at AVO factory at South Ockendon)

Engine

Type	Four cylinders, in line, with twin overhead camshaft cylinder head, and four valves per cylinder. Cosworth Type BDA design, on Ford block
Bore, stroke & capacity	80.97×77.62 mm $= 1599$ cc (3.19×3.06 in $= 97.6$ cu in) For homologation purposes, usually quoted as: 80.97×77.72 mm $= 1601$ cc (3.19×3.06 in $= 97.7$ cu in) Difference in stroke was merely a build up of production tolerances
Compression ratio	10.0:1
Cylinder head	Aluminium alloy, with cross-flow breathing and individual inlet and exhaust ports (twin ports from each cylinder became one kidney-shaped port at manifold faces). Pent-roof combustion chamber with symmetrically disposed twin inlet and exhaust valves at included angle of 40 degrees. Two camshafts mounted in cylinder head driven by single toothed belt
Cylinder block	(To autumn 1972) Slightly-modified Ford item, combined with crankcase, in thin-wall cast-iron, with no cylinder liners. (From autumn 1972) Special light alloy casting, retaining major Ford dimensions, with steel cylinder liners
Crankshaft	In cast-iron, fully counterweighted, statically and dynamically balanced and carried in five main bearings. No crankshaft damper on standard engine. Vandervell lead-indium bearings
Pistons	Light alloy, with three rings—two compression and one oil scraper
Carburation	Twin horizontal double-choke Weber 40DCOE carburettors, on inlet manifold cast integrally with cylinder head
Power output	120 bhp (DIN) at 6500 rpm; maximum torque 112 lb ft at 4000

125

rpm. Electronic rev-limiter in the distributor set at approximately 6500 rpm

—all other important mechanical and dimensional features were the same as for the Escort Twin-Cam, except for the unladen weight, quoted at 1920 lb (870 kg)

Development changes:
Through the life of the car, mechanical changes (except for the adoption of a light-alloy cylinder block from October 1972) were minor, and amendments to 'chassis' and body were made at the same time as mass-production Escorts were modified. When the light-alloy block was standardised, four-way flashers and sports road wheels were also included in the specification

Basic prices in Great Britain
From

April 1970	£1108	December 1971	£1237	December 1973	£1623
January 1971	£1145	June 1972	£1285	April 1974	£1762
April 1971	£1214	October 1972	£1480	July 1974	£1923
October 1971	£1197	October 1973	£1566	October 1974	£2048

FORD ESCORT MEXICO (MARK I)
Period produced: November 1970 to December 1974
Specification for Escort RS1600 except for

Engine

Type	Four cylinders, in line, with pushrod-operated overhead valve gear, of Ford 'Kent' family
Bore, stroke & capacity	80.97 × 77.62 mm = 1599 cc (3.19 × 3.06 in = 97.6 cu in)—same homologation details as for RS1600
Compression ratio	9.0:1
Cylinder head	Cast-iron, with cross-flow breathing, and individual inlet and exhaust ports. Flat cylinder head face, and combustion chamber contained in dished crown of pistons
Cylinder block	Cast-iron Ford item, as 1970–72 RS1600s. Light-alloy block never offered
Carburation	One downdraught compound dual-choke Weber 32 DFM carburettor, on cast-alloy inlet manifold
Power output	86 bhp (DIN) at 5500 rpm; maximum torque 92 lb ft at 4000 rpm
Unladen weight	1965 lb (891 kg)

Development changes
Mainly as for mainstream Escorts and as for RS1600. However, the battery was re-located

in the boot at the same time as sports wheels and carpeted floors were standardised in October 1972

Basic prices in Great Britain
From

December 1970	£881	June 1972	£1003	April 1974	£1292
April 1971	£934	October 1972	£1072	July 1974	£1410
October 1971	£943	October 1973	£1133	October 1974	£1502
December 1971	£974	December 1973	£1190		

FORD ESCORT RS2000 (MARK I)
Period produced: July 1973 to December 1974

Engine

Type	Four cylinders, in line, with single overhead camshaft cylinder head, and slightly opposed line of valves. Ford 'Pinto' type
Bore, stroke & capacity	90.8 × 76.95 mm = 1993 cc (3.58 × 3.03 in = 121.6 cu in)
Compression ratio	9.2:1
Cylinder head	Cast-iron, with cross-flow breathing, and individual inlet and exhaust ports. Pent-roof combustion chamber, with inlet and exhaust valves symmetrically disposed at included angle of 15 degrees. Single camshaft mounted in cylinder head, driven by one-stage rubber cogged belt
Cylinder block	Cast-iron, combined with crankcase, in thin-wall cast-iron, with no cylinder liners
Crankshaft	In cast-iron, fully counterweighted, statically and dynamically balanced, and carried in five main bearings. No crankshaft damper on standard engine. All bearing shells with copper-lead or aluminium-tin coatings, depending on supplier
Pistons	Light-alloy, flat topped, with solid skirts and three rings— two compression and one oil scraper
Carburation	One downdraught compound dual-choke Weber, on light alloy inlet manifold. (Homologated kit of twin down-draught dual-choke Solex instruments and matching manifold also available)
Power output	100 bhp (DIN) at 5750 rpm; maximum torque 108 lb ft at 3500 rpm. No rev-limiter fitted

Transmission

Type	Four-speed, all-synchromesh, manual gearbox, of Ford design, with remote-control selection and centre gear change

Internal ratios	1.00, 1.37, 1.97, 3.65, reverse 3.66:1
Rear axle	Hypoid bevel, 3.54:1
Propeller shaft	Two-piece, with centre steady bearing

(Note: Alternative gearbox and axle ratios were available for competition purposes)

Chassis and suspension

Type	Pressed-steel unit-construction bodyshell, in two-door saloon car style, modified from normal mass-production Ford Escort design. All structural stress-carrying members built into bodyshell. Twin-Cam/RS1600 style
Front suspension	Independent, by coil springs on MacPherson struts, of same type as Twin-Cam and RS1600
Steering	Rack and pinion, left-hand or right-hand drive
Rear suspension	Live axle, half-elliptic leaf springs, of Twin-Cam/RS1600 type
Wheels and tyres	Pressed-steel wheels, with four fixing studs. 13-in diameter and 5.5-in width. 165-13-in radial ply tyres
Brakes	Disc front brakes, drum rears, hydraulically operated, with servo assistance. 9.62-in front discs, 8 × 1.5-in rear drums. Front swept area 190 sq in, rear swept area 75 sq in; total swept area 265 sq in

Bodywork

Single body style, pressed-steel two-door saloon, of Twin-Cam/RS1600 type, with different paint/decoration styles. Twin-Cam/RS1600 options also available

Major dimensions

As for Twin-Cam and RS1600 models, except for:

Kerb weight (approx)   1975 lb (898 kg)

Development changes
None, as the life of the model was only 18 months

Basic prices in Great Britain:
From

July 1973	Export only	July 1974	£1578
October 1973	£1333	September 1974	£1684
April 1974	£1446		

FORD ESCORT RS1800

Period produced: June 1975 to September 1977 (hand-built examples, homologated as Escort RS, built until 1980)

Engine

Type
Four cylinders, in line, basically Cosworth BDA of alloy-block RS1600 type except for:

Bore, stroke & capacity
86.75 × 77.62 mm = 1835 cc (3.42 × 3.06 in = 111.9 cu in)

Compression ratio
9.0:1

Carburation
Single downdraught compound dual-choke Weber Type 32/36 DGAV carburettor

Power output
115 bhp (DIN) at 6000 rpm; maximum torque 120 lb ft at 4000 rpm

Transmission

Type
Four-speed, all-synchromesh, manual gearbox, of Ford design, with remote-control selection and centre gear change

Internal ratios
1.00, 1.26, 1.81, 3.36, reverse 3.37:1

Rear axle
Hypoid bevel, 3.54:1

Propeller shaft
Two-piece, with centre bearing

Chassis and suspension

Type
All of RS1600 type, including many 'carry-over' items, but topped by Escort Mark II body style, as introduced in January 1975

Major dimensions

Overall width
5 ft 0.5 in (1540 mm)

Overall height
4 ft 7.5 in (1410 mm)

Kerb weight (approx)
2015 lb (915 kg)

Development changes

None, except that the car was originally marketed in standard and 'Custom' trim. The Custom option was dropped at the end of 1976

Basic prices in Great Britain

From

	RS1800	RS1800 'Custom'
July 1975	£2416	£2527
October 1975	£2500	£2606
February 1976	£2625	£2736
May 1976	£2740	£2856
August 1976	£2870	£2992

November 1976	£3010	—
February 1977	£3236	—
May 1977	£3414	—
August 1977	£3654	—

FORD ESCORT RS2000 MARK II
Period produced: January 1976 to September 1980

Engine

Type
Ford 'Pinto' type, basically as fitted to Mark I RS2000, except for:

Power output
110 bhp (DIN) at 5500 rpm; maximum torque 119 lb ft at 4000 rpm

Transmission

Type
As fitted to the RS2000 Mark I

Chassis and Suspension

Type and details
As fitted to the RS2000 Mark I topped by Mark II Escort body style

Wheels
(RS2000 up to autumn 1978, and RS2000 Custom thereafter) Cast-alloy wheels, with four fixing studs. 13-in diameter and 6.0-in rim width
(RS2000 from autumn 1978) Pressed-steel road wheels, with four fixing studs. 13-in diameter and 5.5-in rim width

Brakes
Front discs as Mark I RS2000, rear drums 9×1.75 in. Front swept area 190 sq in., rear swept area 96 sq in. Total swept area 286 sq in

Bodywork

Single body style, pressed-steel two-door saloon, with polyurethane contoured nose-cone, based on body shell of Mark II Escort announced in January 1975

Major dimensions

Wheelbase 7 ft 10.5 in (2400 mm)
Front track 4 ft 2 in (1270 mm)
Rear track 4 ft 3 in (1295 mm)
Overall length 13 ft 7.1 in (4140 mm)
Overall width 5 ft 0.5 in (1540 mm)
Overall height 4 ft 7.5 in (1410 mm)
Kerb weight (approx) 2075 lb (941 kg)

Development changes
No significant mechanical changes. In autumn 1978, however, RS2000 became RS2000 Custom, while cheaper, less well-equipped derivative was also introduced, mechanically identical except for use of steel wheels

130

Basic prices in Great Britain
From
January 1976   £2442
—rising rapidly, at three-monthly intervals, to
June 1978   £3701
In September, the range was revised with two different trim packs being on offer

	RS2000	*RS2000 Custom*
September 1978	£3335	£3774

—again rising rapidly to its final price level

June 1980	£3949	£4466

FORD ESCORT RS MEXICO (MARK II STYLE)
Period produced: January 1976 to August 1978
Basic specification as for RS1800, except for:

Engine

Type   Four-cylinder in-line, of basic RS2000/'Pinto' single overhead camshaft type.

Bore, stroke & capacity 87.65×66 mm = 1593 cc (3.45×2.60 in = 97.2 cu in)

Compression ratio   9.2:1

Carburation   Single downdraught compound dual-choke Weber carburettor

Power output   95 bhp (DIN) at 5750 rpm; maximum torque 92 lb ft at 4000 rpm

Transmission

Internal ratios   1.00, 1.37, 1.97, 3.65, reverse 3.66:1

Rear axle   Hypoid bevel, 3.65:1

Chassis and Suspension

Kerb weight (approx)   1990 lb (902 kg)

Basic prices in Great Britain
January 1976   £2088
—risingly rapidly, at three-monthly intervals, to
June 1978   £3105

FORD ESCORT RS
Period produced: 1975 to 1981 inclusive

This was the special competition derivative of the Escort RS1800 road car, developed by the Ford Competitions Department and homologated for sporting purposes as from 1 April 1977:

131

to qualify for Group 4 homologation, a minimum production of 400 cars in two consecutive calendar 12-month periods had to be achieved. It is not possible to say how many were built as, in addition to those constructed by and on behalf of Ford, hundreds were created by the progressive modification of RS1800s or even by the re-bodying and up-dating of RS1600s.

Compared with the RS1800, however, the Escort RS (its official 'homologation' title) had a 90 × 77.62 mm, 1975 cc BDA engine and twin horizontal dual-choke Weber carburettors (power output depended on the state of tune used), a dry sump lubrication system (with the oil tank in the boot of the car), a five-speed all-synchromesh ZF gearbox, with a choice of internal ratios, a different 'Atlas' back axle with a wide choice of final-drive ratios, and axle location by twin pairs of trailing arms and a Panhard rod.

There were many other differences, including the standardisation of wheel arch extensions, special instrumentation, lightweight seats, and a host of optional extra equipment.

The price of the car depended entirely on which options were specified, and how much extra and alternative equipment was also supplied when the car was built.

Escort—the Competition timetable

Model	Announced	Homologation—date, number, Group	First rally win (International)
Twin-Cam	Jan 1968	Mar 1968, Gp 3	*April 1968 (Circuit)
		May 1968, 1524, Gp 2	May 1968 (Acropolis)
RS1600	Jan 1970	Oct 1970, 1605, Gp 2	*March 1970 (Circuit)
Mexico	Nov 1970	May 1968, 1524, Gp 1	—
RS2000	July 1973	April 1974, 5566, Gp 1	July 1974 (Tour of Britain)
RS1800	Jan 1975	May 1975, 1605, Gp 2	May 1975 (Welsh)
RS2000 (Mark II)	Jan 1976	Jan 1976, 5566, Gp 1	July 1976 (Tour of Britain)
RS Mexico (Mark II)	Jan 1976	April 1976, 5586, Gp 1	—
Escort RS	—	April 1977, 650, Gp 4	April 1977 (Safari)

*As non-homologated prototypes.

Acknowledgements

In effect, if not in fact, it took me 12 years to write this book, for my enthusiasm was kindled by the first of the Twin-Cams in 1968, and I have been an avid Escort-watcher ever since.

My thanks for information supplied, from time to time, go to Stuart Turner and Martyn Watkins of Ford's Public Affairs staff, to John Griffiths of Boreham for his guide to the complexities of the sporting homologation scene and to Mick Jones and Bill Meade for their recollections of the early days of the Twin-Cam project. Keith Duckworth (who *is* Cosworth) told me more about the BDA engine than I could ever have researched and I am also grateful to Peter Ashcroft and Brian Hart for their stories about the birth of the light-alloy BDA unit. Some time ago, too, Walter Hayes spelt out to me the sequence of events leading up to the founding of the Ford Advanced Vehicle Operation.

Paul Gilligan, joint managing director of my local Ford dealership, often set me right in regard to the success or otherwise of the various cars, and I owe a lot to my friends at *Autocar* for recalling their impressions of the various RS models.

Lastly, and by no means least, my undying admiration to Roger Clark, who not only drove the best Escorts faster and more often than almost anyone else in the world, but sold a lot of them too. Roger, more than anyone, showed me how a truly rapid Escort should be driven, and he never lost his enthusiasm for them.

Illustrative help came from the Ford Motor Company's excellent photographic department, Mirco Decet and *Autocar*. Help and encouragement came also from two enthusiast bodies, both recently formed. Roger Bailey, press and publicity officer of The AVO Owners Club catering specifically for the RS1600, Mk 1 Mexico and RS2000 and RS3100 Capri bombarded us with more material than we could use. David Harrison, secretary of the RS Owners Club which takes in all Escort, Capri and Fiesta owners whose cars carry the 'RS' prefix, plus the Twin-Cam and Mexico, added his weight. Thank you all.

Index